Social Partnership and Economic Performance

Social Partnership and Economic Performance

The Case of Europe

Bernard Casey

Robert Schuman Fellow, European Institute, London School of Economics, UK

Michael Gold

Senior Lecturer in European Business and Employee Relations, Royal Holloway College, University of London, UK

Edward Elgar
Cheltenham, UK • Northampton, MA, USA

© Bernard Casey and Michael Gold 2000

Published by
Edward Elgar Publishing Limited
Glensanda House
Montpellier Parade
Cheltenham
Glos GL50 1UA
UK

Edward Elgar Publishing, Inc.
136 West Street
Suite 202
Northampton
Massachusetts 01060
USA

A catalogue record for this book
is available from the British Library

Library of Congress Cataloguing in Publication Data

Casey, Bernard.
    Social partnership and economic performance : the case of Europe / Bernard Casey, Michael Gold.
        Includes bibliographical references.
        1. International relations—Europe—Case studies. 2. Europe—Social policy. 3. Europe—Economic conditions—1945– I. Gold, Michael. II. Title.

HD6657.C345 2000

                                                        99–088522

ISBN 1 84064 200 9

Printed and bound in Great Britain by MPG Books Ltd, Bodmin, Cornwall

Contents

List of Figures and Tables

FIGURE

TABLES

Note on Authors

Bernard Casey is Robert Schuman Fellow at the European Institute, London School of Economics. He has also worked at the Labour Market Policy Research Unit of the Wissenschaftszentrum Berlin (Science Centre Berlin) and, for over ten years, at the Policy Studies Institute in London. He has acted as consultant to the OECD, various UK government departments and the Commission of the EC.

Michael Gold is Senior Lecturer in European Business and Employee Relations at Royal Holloway College, University of London. He worked formerly at Incomes Data Services and at Industrial Relations Services, where he edited the *European Industrial Relations Review*. He is currently consultant editor for the *European Industrial Relations Observatory*.

Abbreviations

Au	Austria
D	Germany
E	Spain
EU	European Union
F	France
I	Italy
Irl	Ireland
NL	Netherlands
Sv	Sweden
UK	United Kingdom
USA	United States of America

AMS	Labour Market Board (Arbetsmarknadsstyrelsen) (Sv)
BDA	Confederation of German Employers' Associations (Bundesvereinigung der Deutschen Arbeitgeberverbände)
BMAGS	Federal Ministry for Labour, Health and Social Affairs (Bundesministerium für Arbeit, Gesundheit und Soziales) (Au)
BoP	Balance of Payments
CAP	Common Agricultural Policy (EU)
CBI	Confederation of British Industry
CCN	National Audit Commission (Commission de la comptabilité nationale) (F)
CCOO	Workers' Commissions (Comisiones Obreras) (E)
CES	Economic and Social Council (Consejo Económico y Social) (E)
CES	Economic and Social Council (Conseil économique et social) (F)

CFDT	French Democratic Confederation of Labour (Confédération française démocratique du travail)
CGdP	National Planning Authority (Commissariat général du plan) (F)
CGT	General Confederation of Labour (Confédération générale du travail) (F)
CNEL	National Council for Economic and Labour Affairs (Consiglio Nazionale dell'Economia e del Lavoro) (I)
CPB	Central Planning Bureau (Centraal Planbureau) (NL)
DGB	German Trade Union Federation (Deutscher Gewerkschaftsbund)
DGV	Directorate-General V (Employment, Industrial Relations and Social Affairs) (EU)
EC	European Communities
ECSC	European Coal and Steel Community (EU)
EIRO	European Industrial Relations Observatory
EIRR	European Industrial Relations Review
EMU	European Monetary Union
ESC	Economic and Social Committee (EU)
ESRI	Economic and Social Research Institute (Irl)
FGÖ	Austrian Free Trade Union (Freie Gewerkschaft Österreichs)
FPÖ	Austrian Freedom Party (Freiheitliche Partei Österreichs)
GDP	Gross Domestic Product
ICTU	Irish Congress of Trade Unions
IRRA	Industrial Relations Research Association (USA)
JSA	Job Security Agreement (UK)
LO	Federation of Trade Unions (Landsorganisationen) (Sv)
MI	Industry Round Table (Mesa de Industria) (E)
MSC	Manpower Services Commission (UK)

NAIRU	Non-accelerating inflationary rate of unemployment
NAP	National Action Plan for Employment (EU)
NEDC	National Economic Development Council (UK)
NESC	National Economic and Social Council (Irl)
NESF	National Economic and Social Forum (Irl)
OECD	Organisation for Economic Co-operation and Development
ÖNB	Austrian Central Bank (Österreichische Nationalbank)
PKLP	Parity Commission for Wages and Prices (Paritätische Kommission für Lohn- und Preisfragen) (Au)
QWL	Quality of Working Life
SAF	Swedish Employers' Confederation (Svenska Arbetsgivareföreningen)
SEM	Single European Market
SER	Social-Economic Council (Sociaal-Ekonomische Raad) (NL)
SPD	German Social Democratic Party (Sozialdemokratische Partei Deutschlands)
STAR	Foundation of Labour (Stichting van de Arbeid) (NL)
SZW	Ministry of Social and Labour Affairs (Ministerie van Sociale Zaken en Werkgelegenheid) (NL)
TEC	Training and Enterprise Council (UK)
TUC	Trades Union Congress (UK)
UGT	General Workers' Confederation (Unión general de trabajadores) (E)
WIFO	Austrian Institute for Economic Research (Österreichisches Institut für Wirtschaftsforschung)

Introduction

This book seeks to assess the impact of forms of social partnership and social protection on the macroeconomic performance of nine member states of the EU: Austria, France, Germany, Ireland, Italy, the Netherlands, Spain, Sweden and the UK. It is divided into four chapters covering definitions and terminology, trends and developments across the nine countries, measures of economic performance and matters arising. The last chapter pays particular attention to the evolution of EU social policy.

The book's approach is necessarily interdisciplinary, drawing on relevant literature in the fields of economics, political science and industrial relations, gathering together much information that cannot be otherwise found in one source.

SUMMARY

Chapter 1 defines social partnership as a set of interactions between the various social partners designed to achieve a forum for the discussion and possibly resolution of joint problems, acknowledging that the methods, levels and forms of these interactions vary widely between countries and over time. It defines social protection as a range of benefits intended to enhance the security of workers both in the labour market and out of it. A basic premise of the analysis is that both 'too little' and 'too much' social partnership and social protection may lead to suboptimal performance, and that the 'right balance' is a matter of empirical enquiry within individual national settings.

The role of social partnership and protection in four areas of the economy – macroeconomic policy, pay determination and employee relations, training and social security – is the subject of Chapter 2. This chapter shows how, over the past decade or so, there has been a trend toward decentralisation and deregulation in policy making and policy implementation in many of the countries typically referred to as 'neo-corporatist'. However, it also shows how central agreements (or 'pacts') covering a range of issues have been concluded in certain countries with less of a neo-corporatist tradition, as governments and economic and social actors have sought to cope with change or crisis.

The analysis of structures and trends in nine countries illustrates the serious difficulties involved in using broad-brush terms – such as 'neo-corporatist', 'statist' or 'free market liberal' – when trying to describe policy approaches and policy-making systems. Common features between countries with respect to any one subsystem (such as industrial relations) do not necessarily match common features between those countries with respect to another subsystem (such as social security). For these reasons the book, in considering outcomes, focuses on the individual country as the most appropriate unit of analysis.

Chapter 3 tries to answer the central question set by the book: what is the impact of social partnership and protection on each country's economic performance? The chapter emphasises that this is a complex task for a number of reasons. First, the direction of causality is not always obvious. Second, lengthy time lags may be expected before 'improved' performance emerges from institutional restructuring. And third, institutions that are functional in certain economic, social or demographic environments may become dysfunctional in others. In addition, the chapter recognises that country-specific 'shocks' may have a major impact on performance, and that not all EU member states are at the same stage of the economic cycle at any particular moment. This means that the time period over which it is appropriate to assess performance may be politically sensitive.

The analysis breaks down the concept of 'performance' into certain component parts, including growth in gross domestic product, the rate of inflation, the rate of unemployment and the external balance. It then compares the outcome for each country, and for the USA, in the light of the institutional trends and developments in social partnership and performance outlined in Chapter 2. The results are by no means always unambiguous, but it seems as if both Austria and Germany have experienced a decline in performance since the 1980s. They are, arguably, the countries that have undergone least formal change in their systems of social partnership and protection. By contrast, Ireland, the Netherlands and Sweden have improved and demonstrate certain common characteristics, namely moves towards what is sometimes called 'supply-side corporatism' as well as ordered deregulation and decentralisation. The UK and the USA have also generally performed well with market-oriented economies, although income inequality has worsened. The benefits of social pacts are harder to assess. Ireland's upturn followed the introduction of national understandings, but similar approaches in Italy and Spain have not yet borne comparable results.

Chapter 4 considers three issues arising from the earlier chapters. These are: social partnership as a dynamic process, its complexity and the difficulty of assessing its impact; the role of EU-level social policy in promoting economic performance; and social partnership as an inclusive process. The first of these is about the relationship between institutions and economic outcomes both in theory and in practice. The second relates to the extent to which EU policy, which has been increasingly stressing the contribution of social partnership, might assist the achievement of those conditions that were identified as being conducive to successful performance. The third issue arises from the debate about how appropriate social partnership is as a means of economic and social policy formulation and asks how, both in individual member states and across the EU as a whole, its representivity might be improved and expanded.

With respect to the first issue – social partnership as a dynamic process – it must be stressed that although terms such as 'social partners' and 'social partnership' are widely used in Europe, their meaning differs greatly depending on the country in question. Social partnership covers negotiation, consultation and information disclosure, all of which may take place at levels ranging from the intersectoral to the workplace. Because of these differences, trying to relate social partnership to national performance is inherently difficult. If such an attempt is to be made at all, then it must be made on a country by country basis, and it needs sensitivity both to causality and to what should be counted as performance. With respect to the second issue – the role of EU social policy – attention is focused on employment promotion, an aspect that has come to dominate recent debates in this area. The chapter reviews the outcomes of recent European Councils and summits and how they have led to agreement on employment guidelines and on a European Employment Pact. It also examines the contribution that the social partners are assumed to make in successfully creating jobs. With respect to the third issue – social partnership as an inclusive process – questions are raised about who is represented in decisions about public policy and how. Partnership that involves only organised capital and organised labour bypasses many important social interests – such as the unemployed, pensioners and consumers – and might also usurp the place of democratically elected government. There is a need to consider the extent to which different forms of social partnership may be seen to add authority to policy-making, and the chapter goes on to review ways in which its legitimacy and effectiveness might be improved.

BACKGROUND TO THE STUDY

This book grew out of work undertaken for the Austrian Federal Ministry for Labour, Health and Social Affairs (BMAGS) to help inform the policymaking process during the Austrian presidency in the second half of 1998. The ministry was keen to test the theory that high levels of social partnership and protection promote economic performance. In order to satisfy the ministry's commission, the authors

- undertook a review of the relevant literature from a range of academic disciplines and processed information sources such as specialist journals dealing with contemporary social, political and economic issues;
- distributed a semi-structured survey amongst national experts to gather information about the most recent developments in social partnership and protection across the nine countries in the study; and
- appraised and analysed data sets containing indicators of 'performance'.

The research on which the book is based involved the assembly of a complex array of information. It is, therefore, important to highlight what it could, and what it could not, reasonably be expected to achieve.

First, it had to be recognised that the subject was potentially vast. The authors were concerned with four broad areas that might be subject to social partnership and recognised that with respect to some of these areas dialogue could occur at many levels. Given that nine countries were to be covered, treatment of the subject had to be selective and also relatively superficial. Only key practices and developments could be reported. Nevertheless, as well as too much information, the authors were occasionally hampered by too little. In particular, consistent data on income distribution were not available for all the countries in the study.

Over and above this, the authors faced two further problems. First, the subject matter required them to use a large number of terms, including 'social partnership', 'corporatism', 'centralisation', 'economic performance' and 'inclusion', the meanings of which were not common to all commentators and observers. The authors have sought to make clear the definitions they use, and to set these alongside the definitions used by certain others. However, they often felt uneasy about applying certain terms to certain countries. They also recognised that, even if certain categorisations might once have been relevant, societies and institutions are in constant flux. Indeed, as noted above, this was one of the reasons why the authors used individual countries as the unit of investigation.

Second, even where there was a common denotation – in other words, even if there was agreement on how to apply certain categories to certain developments – the authors had to deal with the problem of connotation. Terms have emotive or culturally bound meanings as well as 'factual' or 'objective' meanings. For example, in Austria 'corporatism' has a positive ring in that it is associated with economic success over many years, but in the UK the same term carries a pejorative overtone, harking back to the apparent failures of economic policy in the 1970s. Similarly, in Austria, 'inclusion' appears to refer specifically to the coverage of workers through collective agreements or pension schemes, but in the UK the term currently appears to refer to the integration of those people left outside – or excluded from – the labour market, such as the unemployed and pensioners. Although it seems as if a common language is being used, it has to be recognised that discourse is multicultural and multifaceted and hides many pitfalls for the unwary.

In consequence, different observers have different perceptions about situations and their development. For example, in making initial presentations to the Austrian government, the authors described the particular form of social partnership in that country as 'relatively unchanging' over the 1980s and 1990s. They did so because it seemed to them that the relevant institutions had undergone only rather minor changes by comparison with those observed in social partnership institutions in other EU member states. However, the view of the Austrian ministry was very different. In Austria, what the authors saw as minor changes were perceived as significant changes, and this reflected the way in which these changes had been experienced in that country. This critical point is well expressed by Gunnar Myrdal, who wrote in the early 1950s:

> Once one has grown accustomed to thinking within the frame of the inherited normative system, which offers the assurance of a 'beaten track', it becomes difficult to step aside and inspect the system from the outside, in the same way as it is difficult for creatures living two-dimensional lives on the surface of a sphere, to cite Einstein's famous example, to suspect the existence of a third dimension. (Myrdal, 1953: 22)

All those who engage in cross-cultural or cross-national research and policy making have to cultivate this ability to step outside their own 'beaten tracks'. This book seeks to meet that aspiration by presenting as accurate and as sensitive an analysis as possible. The authors hope that, by doing this, they will lay the groundwork for further debate amongst policy makers and practitioners.

ACKNOWLEDGEMENTS

The authors gratefully acknowledge the contribution of the following people in completing the experts' survey on recent developments in social partnership and protection: Austria: Brigitte Unger (Wirtschafts-universität, Vienna); France: Alexandre Bilous (IRES, Paris); Ireland: Brendan MacPartlin (National College for Industrial Relations, Dublin); Italy: Serafino Negrelli (Fondazione Regionale Pietro Seveso, Milan); Spain: María Caprile (CIREM, Barcelona) and Clara Llorens (QUIT, Barcelona); Sweden: Klas Levinson (Arbetslivsinstitutet, Stockholm). The German and Dutch surveys were completed by Bernard Casey and the UK survey by Bernard Casey and Michael Gold. These surveys were supplemented by material drawn from the *European Industrial Relations Observatory* and the *European Industrial Relations Review*, both valuable sources of information on key areas covered by this book.

The authors would also like to thank all members of the international advisory committee to the Austrian Federal Ministry of Labour, Health and Social Affairs for their helpful and patient comments, and particularly Birgit Stimmer for her work in co-ordinating the project.

They appreciate as well the assistance of the following: Birgit Benkhoff, John Evans, August Gaechter, Alois Guger, Franz Gundacker, Bob Hanke, Dick Moraal, Wouter Roorda, David Soskice, Sig Vitols and Els Vogels. The publisher's anonymous referee provided a set of reflective comments on the initial draft, which were also greatly appreciated.

However, the authors alone are responsible for any errors of commission or omission.

Bernard Casey and Michael Gold
September 1999

1 Social Partnership, Social Protection and Economic Performance

Throughout much of the 1990s, academics and politicians sought to draw comparisons between the economic success of the United States of America and the relative failure of Europe. Commentators have focused in particular on labour market conditions where contrasts between the two are most apparent. America is seen as a job creation machine, exemplified by the increase in the numbers at work. Over the period 1985–95, the average increase in employment was 1.5 per cent a year in the USA but only 0.4 per cent across the member states of the European Union. Similarly, the unemployment rate in the USA fell from nearly 7 per cent in 1991 to less than 5 per cent in 1997. In comparison, the EU unemployment rate had risen from 8 per cent to over 10 per cent over the same period. Of course, such a characterisation is a partial one because, as this book will point out, there are many other ways of measuring performance. Nevertheless, rates of employment and unemployment are significant indicators of economic and social well-being.

This book is concerned with economic performance in Europe and with the institutions in Europe that contribute to or detract from it. In particular it is concerned with those institutions that differentiate Europe from the USA. In Europe, for example, organisations representing business and employees have a greater influence – in appearance if not always in practice – over the processes of policy formulation and execution than their counterparts in the USA. Furthermore, the state in European countries plays a more important role in the regulation of employment relationships and in the provision of income replacement for those temporarily or permanently unable or too old to work. One of the more obvious indicators of these differences is the higher rate of collective bargaining coverage in Europe than in the USA. In 1994 this ranged in Europe from 98 per cent in Austria down to 47 per cent in the UK. Yet in the same year the USA recorded a mere 18 per cent coverage. Another indicator is the higher share of national income accounted for by public social insurance and means-tested benefits – some 28 per cent in Europe compared with 15 per cent in the USA.

The institutions associated with such forms of collective representation and collective provision can be conceptualised in the terms 'social partnership' and 'social protection'. Their more precise form and content will be discussed later. Here, it is sufficient to say that some commentators argue that their existence, form and significance have a certain impact upon the performance of countries. On the one hand, there are those who suggest that degrees of social partnership and social protection explain at least partly the 'superior' performance of the USA, where they are relatively under-important, and the 'inferior' performance of Europe, where they are relatively over-important. On the other hand, there are those who seek to defend what is now increasingly referred to as the 'European social model'. This model, which has been described as 'a number of shared values which ... include democracy and individual rights, free collective bargaining, the market economy, equality of opportunity for all and social welfare and solidarity' (Commission, 1994a: 2, para. 3), is clearly predicated upon the maintenance of social partnership and social protection.

The Dutch presidency of the European Union, in the first part of 1997, devoted considerable energy to propagating the view that social protection was a productive factor, and dedicated a major conference and a series of publications to this (see, particularly, SZW, 1997). The Austrian presidency of the second half of 1998 sought not only to build on the work carried out under the Dutch presidency, but also, since Austria was a new member state, to propagate Austria's singular form of policy formulation – one based upon social partnership (BMAGS, 1998; Hostasch, 1998).[1] Within the Commission itself, the Directorate-General for employment, industrial relations and social affairs (DGV) clearly subscribes to the view that there are positive returns to social policy, as its Communication, *Modernising and Improving Social Protection* (1997a), makes clear. In the USA, interest appears more academic, but the Industrial Relations Research Association devoted considerable space to discussion of lessons from Europe at its June 1999 national conference at which the Director General of DGV was a keynote speaker.[2]

Of course, on both sides of the Atlantic there are still those who analyse the 'root cause' of 'Europe's severe structural problems' in terms of 'the continent's deeply entrenched social contract' and its associated costs – in particular, high payroll taxes and restrictive labour market practices (Roach, 1998). It is also the case that finance ministries are much more inclined to share this analysis than their labour and social ministry counterparts, which are generally more sympathetic to concepts of social partnership and protection. Yet this is scarcely surprising since finance ministries levy the taxes which partially pay for them and shoulder overall responsibility for the size of the public sector and the share of national income which flows through the state. They are therefore the ones that stand under political and economic pressure to minimise taxes and the size of the public sector.

This chapter opens by providing an overview of the arguments that have been used to explain why and how institutions of social partnership and social protection can make a contribution to economic performance. For the purposes of analysis, it accepts the presumption that there is an identifiable European social model and outlines its presumed characteristics and advantages, whilst at the same time recognising that the term is an oversimplification. The chapter then explains the principal concepts that are employed in the study and the various uses of certain key terms. Using these concepts and terms, a sketch of the countries covered in the book is given. Lastly, the chapter explains why the individual countries, rather than any broader groupings of countries based upon political, economic or welfare state characteristics, are taken as the unit for further analysis. This is because there are in fact wide variations between EU member countries, which are by no means homogeneous in either their institutions or their performance.

1.1   THEORETICAL FOUNDATIONS OF THE EUROPEAN SOCIAL MODEL

Theoretical foundations to the European social model may be found in the 'new institutional economics' which emphasise transaction costs and their minimisation (Coase, 1988a; Williamson, 1993).

Coase has defined such costs as follows: 'In order to carry out a market transaction, it is necessary to discover who it is that one wishes to deal with, to inform people that one wishes to deal and on what terms, to conduct negotiations leading up to a bargain, to draw up the contract, to undertake the inspection needed to make sure that the terms of the contract are being observed, and so on. These operations are often extremely costly' (Coase, 1988b: 114).

The point is that each of these processes – identifying a dealer, providing relevant information, conducting negotiations and so on – involves time, effort and expense and will itself be the product of customs, traditions, rules and laws embedded in complex institutional arrangements. However, such arrangements may also provide ways for *reducing* some of the costs of complex economic and social interaction where explicit contracts are likely to be inadequate and actors have to rely on the discretion of others. Institutions, both formal and informal, cannot be wished away, although they might be subject to adaptation. Although 'institutions' can frustrate performance by frustrating 'markets', they can also enhance performance once it is recognised that they embody discretion as a value. Furthermore, concentration on short-term advantage by any one player in a 'game' can lead not only to the short-term disadvantage of the other player but also to the long-term disadvantage of both.[3] The new institutional economics therefore stress the importance of ongoing relationships, consensus building and trust (see also Eichengreen, 1996). In political science and sociology, one finds similar concepts employed by those who discuss the importance of 'social capital' – that 'set of institutionalised expectations that other social actors will reciprocate co-operative overtures' (Boix and Posner, 1998: 686).[4]

With respect to employment relationships, where it finds particular application, this approach rejects an analysis predicated upon 'principals' and 'agents', whereby pay and conditions are seen as determined by competition on a 'spot market'. The approach understands rather that exchanges have the potential to be, and indeed usually are, 'dyadic' – that is, that behaviour is determined by anticipation of future outcomes as well as by the expectation of advantage. Accordingly, the institutions that promote such behaviour can be regarded as productive and the expenditures associated with them can be viewed not as costs but as investments.

Within the workplace, institutions that encourage 'voice' – that is, the opportunity to express views and negotiate outcomes – are potentially productivity enhancing. Accordingly, they arguably shift the labour demand curve to the right, thereby offsetting any upward shift of the labour supply curve which unionisation conventionally implies. The productivity enhancing effects of partnership and joint regulation in the enterprise, as frequently argued with respect to the German[5] system of co-determination, are seen to be its contribution to:

- stabilising the qualifications structure by underlining and unifying standards of skill;
- ensuring steady innovation and concentration in the high-quality, high-value added sectors;
- controlling 'shirking' on the employees' side;
- bringing specific problem-solving knowledge/expertise to the management of production and production change; and
- encouraging high flexibility within the enterprise.

Prima facie, organisations that adopt such a regulatory approach might be expected to perform better, for example by showing superior profitability and/or growth, than those that do not. Similarly, countries in which such an approach predominates might be expected to outperform – that is, have higher levels of income – those that do not (for a specific discussion of the German case, at micro and macro level, see respectively Bertelsmann Stiftung/Hans-Böckler-Stiftung, 1998; and Soskice, 1990). Furthermore, institutions that guarantee encompassing wage setting ensure that all parties involved in the bargaining process are aware of their actions and so help to avoid inflationary pay spirals.

Expenditure on training is also, according to such an approach, as much of an investment as the acquisition of physical capital, whether or not it is treated as such in company or national accounts. However, investment in human capital can also encompass provision for improvements to working conditions ('humanisation of labour'), and, along the lines suggested above, this also can be viewed as performance enhancing.

Voluntary provision of welfare benefits by an employer can be understood as the equivalent of paying an 'efficiency wage' that is compensated for in higher levels of commitment. Deferred compensation in the form of a vested pension (one to which the employee has any entitlement at all only after several years' service) or a back-loaded, defined benefit pension (one which pays benefits disproportionately reflecting earnings late in life) discourages 'shirking' and encourages long-term relationships and the acquisition of specific skills. Mandated benefits, such as those provided by state social insurance systems, are frequently treated as a cost to employers, in so far as these are contributors, but employers can equally be regarded as indirect beneficiaries. The costs of the 'de-commodification' of labour (*pace* Goldthorpe, 1984) – that is the costs of sheltering those in the labour market from the worst of the risks associated with work by guaranteeing an acceptable replacement income in cases of sickness, unemployment and old age – can be argued as investment costs rather than, as is often the case, current spending with a zero return, in so far as:

- 'de-commodified' labour is more productive than commodified labour, since it can devote itself to work rather than self-protection;
- workers are not obliged to work when temporarily disabled and thus can recoup their productive power rather than endangering it by continued effort;
- workers assured of acceptable levels of compensation in the event of job loss are more willing to accept technological and structural change; and
- the availability of adequate compensation in case of job loss promotes more efficient matching between the unemployed worker and the new job.

Over and above this, social insurance is generally less expensive than private insurance as it has lower administration costs largely because of savings on marketing and collection costs. Furthermore, private insurance might fail to cover adequately all the risks that social insurance does because of adverse selection, myopia and information asymmetries, with a consequence that the level of protection is lower than the socially optimal level (Barr, 1992).

As well as adding to the productivity of the individual worker who is insured, social protection and social partnership might be defended as necessary infrastructural costs which societies have to bear. There are many who would suggest that unemployment has costs that are greater than the foregone production, if any, of those unemployed, and should include costs of crime induced by the lack of activity or the lack of resources of those without jobs (for a review, see Casey, 1998). There are also many who would argue that, in the face of serious inequalities and poverty amongst a substantial share of the population, social cohesion in the broader sense would be threatened. There is accordingly a case for the provision of such 'public goods' as active labour market policies, and for redistribution. In the absence of such 'symbolic politics', the environment for economic activity would be less stable (Gilbert, 1998).

Equally, it is widely argued that economic success and democracy run hand in hand, or at least, that capitalism is weakened in the absence of a democratic context (UNDP, 1990). Thus, a productive society would have to tolerate institutions that granted its members an adequate degree of both political and economic citizenship. It is to be noted that these arguments are founded upon there being extrinsic as much as intrinsic values to partnership and protection. The state has a role to play in ensuring that certain social standards are maintained, in exactly the same way as it has a role to play in providing law and order and defence. It is acknowledged to be the monopoly provider with respect to the latter, whilst with respect to the former it also has a guarantor role, ensuring basic, minimum standards.

The link between social partnership or protection and economic performance is an unclear one, however, even in its own terms. Like the 'Laffer curve' of 20 years ago, it implies a relationship that in its most basic sense is incontestable, but also a relationship that is so general that it is of little help. The Laffer curve analysis demonstrates that a zero rate of taxation will produce zero tax receipts and equally that a 100 per cent rate of taxation will also produce zero tax receipts, and that there is some optimum rate of taxation in between that will maximise tax receipts. Similarly, it is clear that

- whilst the complete absence of partnership/dialogue is likely to result in suboptimal performance due to high transaction costs and lack of cohesion, too much partnership/dialogue may result in the establishment of procedures which discourage the entertaining of radical alternatives and encourage an over-concern with the interests of 'insiders' (such as current employees of the firm or nationals) to the detriment of the interests of 'outsiders' (such as the unemployed or foreign workers). It may also lead to an excessive concentration on questions of distribution to the detriment of profits and thus of investment and employment (Freeman and Lazear, 1995); and

- whilst the complete absence of social protection can divert workers' attention and undermine their commitment to the social system of which they are a part, too much social protection can result in a lack of willingness to engage in paid work and in excessive costs which destroy employment and the preparedness to invest (Lindbeck et al., 1994).

Furthermore, it is not only the 'quantity' of partnership/dialogue or protection that counts, but also its 'quality'. Where the principal actors are sufficiently encompassing, they are conscious of externalities and avoid behaviour that damages the interests of the whole population. However, there is a – perhaps inevitable – tendency for encompassing organisations to 'devolve' (Olson, 1995, 1996) into mere coalitions of their parts, each with narrower interests and with less respect for any 'general interest' in their pursuit of these narrower interests. There is, equally, a danger that encompassing organisations become over-confident in their pursuit of what they identify as a public good, placing strains upon the economy, or promoting perverse incentives that cannot in the longer run be tolerated.

Whilst it is easy to suggest that an 'optimal' level of social partner-ship and protection exists, determining when it has been reached is an empirical problem that is by no means easy to resolve. Ultimately, the discussion is not one of absolutes but one of marginal increments and decrements. In other words, it is not one of whether there should be social partnership and protection at all, but of whether there is too much here, or too little there, and of what changes, in what direction, would be beneficial. This is not to say that the discussion is not ideological, since in both the political and the academic arena there are partisans. However, it is to stress that in most cases answers are being sought to rather specific questions, and that there will be lack of unanimity about what these answers are and how they are arrived at.

1.2   DEFINITIONS AND TERMS

This book examines the contribution of social partnership/dialogue and social protection to the economic performance of selected member countries of the European Union. A necessary initial step is, therefore, a definition of the terms 'social partnership', 'social dialogue' and 'social protection' and their various dimensions as they will be used. Moreover, since the study frequently uses the language of the literature of 'new institutionalism', 'varieties of capitalism' and 'the welfare state', a further term – 'corporatism' – also requires some clarification.

Social partnership comprises co-operation between key players in the making of economic and social policy. In particular countries and at particular times, this co-operation might refer mainly or wholly to wage fixing, in other countries and at other times it might embrace a much wider range of topics from management of the economy to provision for retirement. In addition, in different countries, at different times, and according to the scope of the issues upon which co-operation is sought, the key actors might comprise a narrower or wider spectrum. Employers, unions and government agencies are typically regarded as social partners, though representatives of small businesses and the self-employed might be included, as might representatives of other, conventionally more peripheral but none the less important groups such as the unemployed, pensioners and consumers.

Social dialogue can, and often does, involve the same key players as social partnership. However, it is more limited in its ambition and covers merely a structured exchange of views and formal opportunities for consultation rather than co-operation in policy making. In practice, the terms 'partnership' and 'dialogue' are often used synonymously to refer to a set of interactions between employers, unions and possibly government and other social groups, at European Union and individual member state level. Such interactions are designed to achieve at least a forum for discussion of joint problems and at most agreement on the details as well as the broad parameters of policy.

Social protection refers to a range of benefits, such as unemployment compensation and pensions, which enhance the security of workers both when in work and when temporarily or permanently out of the labour market, but also to regulations which govern conditions of work, particularly dismissal procedures. The formulation of such regulations, as well as of benefits policy, might be subject to partnership or dialogue procedures. Equally, the administration of protection might be subject to joint overview, at the national level through agencies subject to bipartite or tripartite boards, and at the workplace level through works councils or union-management committees.

In this book, consideration is given to methods, level, form and status of partnership and dialogue and to its scope or subject areas. These terms also need definition.

Method refers to whether the process is one of mere information disclosure or whether it involves broader forms of influence, ranging from consultation and negotiation to joint decision making and codetermination. The relationship between these different methods may become problematic at the edges. For example, joint consultation committees might be transformed, following union pressure, into joint negotiating committees. Similarly, in countries with statutory works councils, disagreement may centre on whether or not a specific issue is to be settled through consultation or co-determination. Dialogue can also take a variety of forms. It can be tripartite, involving government as well as representatives of business and unions, or even multipartite, involving a wide range of social groups. Form is likely, in part, to be a function of subject matter.

Dialogue and partnership can operate at more than one level of the economy and society. At national or intersectoral level, partnership is concerned with issues that potentially touch all businesses or employees, pensioners, consumers or the unemployed. Since the early 1990s social pacts have been negotiated between governments and social partners in a number of EU member states covering not just labour market issues but also areas like social security contributions and taxation. However, sectoral level dialogue is more likely to be restricted to issues of industrial relations and employment relationships. So, too, is company level and workplace level dialogue. Social partner influence may well vary considerably between levels, depending on political traditions and the nature of industrial relations systems. Some countries in Europe are heavily centralised and/or statist; others are more federal. Some industrial relations systems are based on negotiations at sectoral or even intersectoral levels and others on activity at the level of the individual workplace. To some extent this is a function of the legal framework within which labour relations are settled; to some extent it might also reflect differing degrees of union density.

In some countries dialogue has a statutory basis; in others, custom and practice play a determining role. Thus, the status of dialogue may be formal or informal, and it might be located at any place on a spectrum between these two extremes, such as when it is regulated by renewable collective agreements. Status and level may well interact, although the actual process of interaction is likely to be country specific. As much influence may be exercised through informal channels as through formal channels, especially if the former have become embedded in the dialogue process.

Focusing on one method, form, level or status of dialogue may lead to the serious risk that a significant aspect of social reality is being missed. For this reason, this book adopts as wide an understanding as possible. It accepts that a spectrum of arrangements is compatible with good economic performance and acknowledges, along with the European Commission in its exposition of the outcome of the 1997 Luxembourg Jobs Summit, that the notion of an appropriate level for action will vary from one country to another (Commission, 1997c: 11).

Lastly, it has to be emphasised that the subject matter of dialogue will vary between countries and between levels of dialogue. Pay and working time may be determined at all levels, but aspects of macroeconomic policy or social security will be issues only at intersectoral level, with the interests of government at stake. However, different aspects of the same issue may well be dealt with at different levels. For example, a reduction in working time may be agreed in principle at intersectoral or sectoral level though details of its implementation may be left to the social partners at company or workplace level.

Discussion of social partnership/dialogue almost inevitably leads to discussion of corporatism. The usefulness of this term is discussed at greater length elsewhere in this study (see Chapter 3). As defined in its most general terms, corporatism denotes the presence of structures through which organised interests – particularly labour and capital – participate in the policy formulation process and so gain responsibilities for securing compliance to the decisions thereby made (Grant, 1996). Many writers contrast 'corporatist' with 'statist' systems, where the state takes a central/dirigiste role, market forces are not always predominant and interest groups not particularly strong, and 'market-oriented' systems, where the role of both government and organised interests is relatively limited.

Frequently used as a synonym for corporatism is the term 'neo-corporatism' which is employed to distinguish a current style of governance from one which flourished in certain countries in an earlier period – especially Austria, Germany, Italy, Portugal and Spain – that can be called 'authoritarian corporatism' (Schmitter, 1974). Corporatism or neo-corporatism has two very distinct roots, one lying in catholic social philosophy and emphasising the mutual dependence of labour and capital, and the other lying in social democracy and its interest in planning. However, both 'catholic corporatism' and 'social democratic corporatism', and, indeed, authoritarian corporatism too, may be regarded as 'third', or 'middle' ways, in that they are used to distinguish systems which serve to legitimise the aspirations of organised labour whilst maintaining the capitalist mode of production.

As well as differentiating corporatism according to its ideological underpinning, it can also be differentiated according to its strength. Unger (1998), summarising much recent debate, refers to 'strong', 'intermediate' and 'weak' corporatism. This gradation refers to the density of organisation of critical interest groups and organisations, particularly associations of business and of employees, to the subject matter with which they concern themselves and to the strength of their influence in the policy formulation process.

A further differentiation of corporatism is to be found in some of the more recent writing (see particularly Visser and Hemerijck, 1997) between 'demand-side' and 'supply-side' corporatism. The former, which might be deemed more traditional, describes structures and processes whereby peak associations are involved, in the first instance, in efforts to regulate macroeconomic variables, either (and most commonly) with respect to the overall level of wage and price movements or the levels of government expenditure. The latter, a term referring to more recent developments, describes structures in which the preoccupation of individual businesses and representatives of their workforces with microeconomic variables relating to the performance of specific organisations and companies is given more prominence.

1.3   THE COUNTRIES STUDIED

This book is concerned with the experiences in nine European Union member states over the past two decades. The countries included were selected to provide a mixture of large and small states and northern European and southern European states and on the basis of the authors' initial acquaintance with developments in the economic and social policymaking process and outcomes over time. The countries selected were, in alphabetical order: Austria, France, Germany, Ireland, Italy, the Netherlands, Spain, Sweden and the United Kingdom. In addition, and for limited purposes only, reference is made to the United States of America. The general characteristics, but not the 'performance', of the ten countries, and changes in these, is described in the three tables below.

Table 1.1 summarises the governance styles of each country. By 'governance' is meant the institutional arrangements which control or order relationships between actors, either as groups or as individuals and which determine their rights, expectations and obligations. In particular, the table tries to capture the ways in which economic and social policy is formulated.

The broad terms used mean that what are often considered rather different types of country may receive the same kind of designation. For example, the designation of Germany as most recently 'weak corporatist' does not mean that it necessarily resembles Italy, which is similarly designated in the 1960s to 1980s. It means only that both countries revealed characteristics of weak corporatism within their *own* institutional frameworks over these periods. However, as the final column of Table 1.1 makes clear, there has also been a degree of convergence between certain countries, so that corporatist approaches have weakened in some where they were previously stronger and have emerged in others where they were previously scarcely existent. Chapter 2 describes these developments in greater detail.

Table 1.2 outlines the main features of the social protection systems in each of the countries. As with Table 1.1, summarisation necessarily means that Table 1.2 is a simplification. Unlike Table 1.1, Table 1.2 shows fewer trends. However, it does indicate that in all countries there has been some degree of retrenchment in social protection and

Table 1.1 Form of governance in selected countries

	1960s–70s	1980s	Most recent	Trend
Austria	Centralised, strong corporatist	Centralised, strong corporatist	Centralised, strong corporatist	Relatively unchanging
Sweden	Centralised, strong corporatist	Centralised, strong corporatist	Intermediate corporatist	Decline of corporatism, extension of markets
Netherlands	Strong corporatist	Intermediate corporatist	Intermediate corporatist	Move to supply-side corporatism and markets
Germany	Intermediate corporatist	Intermediate corporatist	Weak corporatist	Decline of corporatism/ consensus
UK	Weak corporatist	Market oriented	Market oriented	Rejection of corporatism
France	Statist	Statist	Statist	Relatively unchanging
Italy	Weak corporatist	Weak corporatist	Experimenting with pacts	Experimenting with pacts
Spain	Authoritarian corporatist	Experimenting with pacts	Experimenting with pacts	Experimenting with pacts
Ireland	Market oriented	Experimenting with pacts	Intermediate corporatist	Embracing neo-corporatism
USA	Market oriented	Market oriented	Market oriented	Unchanged

Note: 'Centralised' means that a high score was given by the OECD for the prevailing wage bargaining level/degree of co-ordination of collective bargaining.

Source: Derived from Unger, 1998 (Table 33, p. 156) and OECD, 1997c (Table 3.3).

that in all of them means-testing has become more prevalent. Some of the explanations for the retrenchments, and the manner in which they have been achieved, are given in Chapter 2.

Table 1.3 captures a specific aspect of each of the countries, namely income distribution. Income distribution, as discussed later (Chapter 3), can be regarded as an 'outcome', and thus as an element of performance, but also as an 'input', since it, along with forms of governance and the welfare state, sets parameters within which policy makers can act. Both the level of inequality and the direction in which inequality is proceeding have implications for legitimacy and therefore for the kind of outcomes which might be tolerated.

The construction of Table 1.3 proved extremely difficult, partly because none of the major data sets contains usable data on all of the countries included. Accordingly, the table should be taken as indicative of broad patterns and trends – as summarised in the final two columns – rather than as giving definitive values. However, it does indicate three broad types of country: those with a relatively egalitarian distribution; those with an intermediate distribution; and those with an unequal distribution of pre-transfer incomes.

1.4   THE UNIT OF INVESTIGATION

At the start of this book, the discussion was pitched in terms of Europe versus the United States of America, though strong reservations as to the homogeneity of the entity entitled Europe were expressed. Tables 1.1 to 1.3 only confirm how appropriate these reservations are. Any study of the contribution of social partnership and social protection to economic performance within an institutional approach needs to have units of analysis, but ones as simple as Europe on the one hand and the USA on the other are unlikely to be helpful. Alternative and prima facie more sophisticated attempts at categorisation are to be found in the literature on 'varieties of capitalism' (such as Albert 1991; Hodges and Woolcock 1993; Thurow 1993; Van Waarden, 1997). In this literature, countries are grouped amongst other factors according to their systems of corporate governance, industrial relations, policy formulation and welfare provision.

Table 1.2 Principal features of social protection in selected countries

Country	Past	Current	Trend
Austria CC	Proportional/insurance-based Generous	Proportional/insurance-based Generous	Minor retrenchments
Sweden SDU	Proportional/insurance-based Redistributive underpin Generous	Proportional/insurance-based Redistributive underpin Generous	Retrenchments
Netherlands CC/SDU	Proportional/insurance-based Redistributive underpin Generous	Proportional/insurance-based Redistributive underpin Generous Private complements	Retrenchments Increased importance placed on private complements
UK LR	Redistributive (flat rate) Ungenerous (need for means-tested supplements for many receiving only basic payments) Substantial private complements	Redistributive (flat rate) Ungenerous (need for means-tested supplements for many receiving only basic payments) Substantial private complements	Substantial retrenchments Increased importance placed on private complements
Germany CC	Proportional/insurance-based Generous	Proportional/insurance-based Generous	Small retrenchments
France CC	Proportional/insurance-based Generous	Proportional/insurance-based Generous Extension of means-tested backups	Small retrenchments of insurance system, extension of means-tested backups

			Retrenchments
Italy CC/LatR	Insurance-based Generous Limited unemployment benefit except in case of redundancy Reliance on family support as well as means-tested benefits as backup	Insurance-based Generous Limited unemployment benefit except in case of redundancy Reliance on family support as well as means-tested benefits as backup	
Spain CC/LatR	Proportional/insurance-based Generous Reliance on family support as well as means-tested benefits as backup Transition from pre-democratic/authoritarian corporatist structure	Proportional/insurance-based Generous Reliance on family support as well as means-tested benefits as backup	Construction of structures appropriate to democratic, industrialised society Adjustments including minor retrenchments
Ireland LR	Redistributive (flat rate) Ungenerous Limited private complements Construction of structures appropriate to industrialised society	Redistributive (flat rate) Ungenerous Limited private complements	Increased importance placed on private complements
USA LR	Proportional/insurance-based Reasonably generous redistributive underpin Substantial private complements No universal health insurance Limited means-tested assistance	Proportional/insurance-based Reasonably generous redistributive underpin Substantial private complements No universal health insurance Restricted means-tested assistance	Retrenchments of means-tested assistance

Note: CC = Conservative–Corporatist; SDU = Social Democratic–Universalist; LR = Liberal–Residual (based upon Esping-Andersen, 1990 typology); LatR = Latin Rim (based upon Ferrara, 1996 typology)

Table 1.3   *Income inequality (Gini coefficients) in selected countries*
            (households, pre-transfer)

	Late 1970s	Late 1980s	Most recent	Trend	Current
Austria	0.32	0.32	0.36	Worsening lately	Medium egalitarian
Sweden	0.27	0.26	0.31	Worsening lately	Egalitarian
Netherlands	0.31	0.31	0.34	Worsening lately	Egalitarian
Germany	0.33	0.32	0.33	Stable	Egalitarian
UK	0.37	0.42	0.50	Still worsening	Unequal
France	0.37	0.35	0.37	Stable	Medium egalitarian
Italy	0.37	0.33	0.34	Improving earlier	Egalitarian
Spain	0.37	0.33	0.34	Improving earlier	Egalitarian
Ireland	0.40	0.44	0.44	Worsened earlier	Unequal
USA	0.38	0.43	0.48	Still worsening	Unequal

Source: Data for the late 1980s taken from Tabatabai, 1996, except for:
- Sweden, which is derived by calculating the average of the ratio of Sweden to the Netherlands, Germany, France and Italy;
- Ireland, which is derived by calculating the average of the ratio of Ireland to the UK and the USA, using the Gini coefficients given in Atkinson, 1995 (Table 4.4); and
- Austria, which is estimated to be approximately the same as Germany on the basis of Atkinson 1995 (Table 4.3).

Data for the late1970s and the most recent period were calculated from Burniaux et al., 1998 (Table 2.2) using mid-points, except for:
- Ireland, where the calculation was based on Collins and Kavanagh, 1998 (Table 9.4); and
- Spain, which is derived from Tabatabai, 1996 and from estimates in Recio and Roca, 1998.

One particular application of this approach is based on the 'three worlds of welfare capitalism' (Esping-Andersen, 1990). Such an approach is helpful in identifying certain of the determining charac-teristics of subsystems; indeed, it was used for the construction of Tables 1.1 and 1.2. However, it is difficult in practice to construct a satisfactory classification that permits all OECD or European Union countries to be ordered into one of three or four types. Countries that can be grouped together with respect, say, to their industrial relations subsystems cannot always be grouped together with respect, say, to their social security and social assistance subsystems. Moreover, where attempts have been made to group countries with respect to any one of these subsystems, closer inspection reveals as much heterogeneity as homogeneity. Even a cursory examination of Tables 1.1 and 1.2 makes this clear.

An example of the first problem – that is, lack of correspondence between subsystems – is the way in which countries like Austria, Germany, Italy and France, which have broadly similar insurance-based and relatively generous social security systems, have remarkably different industrial relations systems. The degree of union density is low in France, but relatively high in Italy and Austria. The degree of co-ordination of collective bargaining is high in Austria, and to a somewhat lesser extent high in Germany, but in France, and traditionally in Italy, it is much lower. The legal and organisational basis and the responsibilities and coverage of workplace representative systems are also very different between Austria and Germany and Italy and France.

An example of the second problem – that is, characterising countries as similar when they are not – is the difference between the United Kingdom and the United States. Both countries are commonly referred to as having 'liberal residual' (*pace* Esping-Andersen, 1990) social protection systems, which are suggested to be relatively ungenerous and supplemented by occupational or private provision. However, with respect to public pensions, the American system is comparatively generous and follows relatively conventional insurance principles whilst the British system is relatively ungenerous and highly redistributive. Nevertheless, in the United Kingdom there is a comprehensive, universal health insurance system, whilst in the United States there is none, and whilst many people in employment gain coverage from their employer, there is a substantial minority of the population which has no health insurance cover at all.

A further problem is that the groupings adopted tend to be static rather than dynamic. Thus, they seldom take account of changes in structure. For example, many analysts of the relationship between wage fixing and performance use an index of 'centralisation' or co-ordination influenced by the work on indices by Calmfors and Driffill (1988). However, not only is there debate between analysts as to how individual countries are to be scored (Unger, 1998), but also those indices which are used reflect appraisals made at a single point in time, and often a decade and more ago. Over the 1990s, wage fixing in Sweden – once highly centralised – has been subject to decentralisation as it has in many other countries. Meanwhile, however, in certain previously relatively decentralised countries – Italy being a good example (Regalia and Regini, 1998: 467) – it has moved in the opposite direction. An exception to the rather static analysis is a recent OECD study (1997c) that scored union density, centralisation and co-ordination of wage bargaining across three different observation points.

Lastly, the process of grouping fails to take account of the way in which institutions, although they might not change their outward appearance, do change the way in which they behave. For example, the Netherlands has retained institutions that influence wage fixing even though they could arguably have been seen as the root cause of that country's earlier economic malaise. However, these same institutions are now credited with taking the lead in determining 'responsible' settlements and affecting the better co-ordination of wage fixing and other aspects of economic and social policy.

For these reasons this book focuses on the individual country as the unit of investigation. This is not because models *cannot* be devised or because institutional analysis is *limited* to the nation state. As other influential commentators have also pointed out, it happens rather to be a fact that capitalism in the twentieth century has been regulated principally through the nation state and that it has been only at this level 'that societies were able through democratic politics to "talk back" to their economies'. As they put it, 'the nation state simply was the only game in town, like it or not' (Crouch and Streeck, 1997a: 2).

Rather than presenting experiences on a country-by-country basis, this book will proceed, in the first instance, on a thematic basis. It will do so by looking at four broad areas of economic and social policy formulation and at the role in this of social partnership/dialogue. The four areas, which are the subject of the following chapter, are macroeconomic policy; pay determination and employee relations; training and labour market policy; and social security.

NOTES

1. Austria became a member of the EU at the start of 1995 along with Finland and Sweden. It was the first of these three new members to hold the rotating presidency.
2. The conference (June 1999) was entitled National Strategies for Employment Policy: Responding to the Challenges of the 21st Century. The IRRA members' magazine *Perspectives on Work*, which appeared shortly before the conference, carried a number of articles on recent European experience.
3. Here the discussion goes beyond simple cases of 'prisoners' dilemma' to include the development of 'tit-for-tat' strategies in repeated games, whereby good favourable moves are reciprocated by the beneficiary, thus encouraging their repetition (Axelrod, 1982).
4. Some writers lay greater stress on informal relationships (for example, Putnam, 1993), others on more formal ones (for example, Coleman, 1990). Others do not use the term social capital at all, even if they are cited by those who do. Thus, North (1992: 9–10) is able to write about institutions as 'formal rules, informal constraints (norms of behaviour, conventions, self-imposed rules, codes of conduct)' and as being 'the structure that humans impose on their relations with one another'. In his words, 'if institutions are the rules of the game, organisations are the players' and the latter, whether formal or informal, are 'groups of individuals engaged in purposive action'. They include, for example, firms, political parties, trade unions or non-market service providers.
5. Germany is sometimes seen by commentators as standing as a proxy for Europe. Thurow for example contrasts the USA, Japan and the European Community as 'centred around its most powerful country, Germany' (1993: 29).

2 Trends and Developments in Nine Countries

Each of the nine countries studied has its own structures and way of proceeding with the formulation of economic and social policy. This chapter analyses four such principal policy areas, namely macroeconomic policy, pay determination and employee relations, training and social security. For each of these policy areas, Austria and the UK have been selected as the initial points of reference. This is because each country represents a polar extreme of socioeconomic development across the member states of the EU. Tables 1.1–1.3 of Chapter 1 have already summarised some of these differences, highlighting Austria as having most of the features of a strong neo-corporatist system and the UK, at least in the 1980s and much of the 1990s, those of a market-oriented, neo-liberal system.

This chapter therefore begins by outlining the origins of the two countries' approaches and sketching an overview of the relevant institutional frameworks in each. The chapter then examines each of the four principal areas of economic and social policy in turn. Each section accordingly outlines the Austrian and UK approaches before focusing on the similarities and contrasts that are found in the remaining countries. Not all aspects of each country are discussed in detail, because in many of them there is not even an approximate equivalent for all that can be found in Austria and the UK. Instead, particular developments in particular countries are highlighted where these developments have been taken to represent distinguishing aspects of alternative approaches, substantial innovations in approach, or even substantial failures. A final section summarises trends across each of the areas and seeks to identify general patterns.

2.1 FEATURES OF THE AUSTRIAN AND UK APPROACHES

The success of the Austrian economy over recent years – measured in terms of growth, low rates of inflation and unemployment and stable industrial relations – may be attributed largely to the country's system of social partnership, a system of co-operation between government, employers and labour across virtually all fields of economic policy. As the OECD has noted, the country's responses to recent challenges in this area have been achieved 'within the framework of public consensus which characterises Austria' (OECD, 1997b: 16). The relative failure of the UK economy – by reference to the same indicators – has equally been attributed to an absence of consensus that reflects deep-seated class divisions and tensions between the different interests of capital and within different sections of the labour movement.

The consensual approach to policy formulation and the development of an accompanying, extensive welfare state was not an automatic development in Austria. Austria experienced considerable turmoil and civil and class conflict during the interwar period culminating in a brief civil war that led to authoritarian rule followed by annexation by Germany. Having been on the losing side of the Second World War, it was occupied and its economy was devastated. It was the need to rebuild a shattered political and economic infrastructure that led to the formation of coalition governments lasting until 1966 and the establishment of the institutions, which persist to this day, of social partnership. Both reflected an acceptance by all democratic actors that only close co-operation between the major parties and organised economic and industrial interests could serve as the foundation for future progress towards peace and prosperity.

In the same way, the UK's approach to economic and social regulation has roots that can be traced back to the industrial revolution of the eighteenth century. Because of its early origins, manufacturing industry in the UK has passed through the full range of production and organisational stages, resulting in the fragmentation both of employers (by production process, use of technology and form of business organisation) and workers (by occupation, status and working practice). Rivalries between trade unions prevented the emergence of the kind of powerful, centralised organisation witnessed notably in the Nordic countries and has ensured that the role of the Trades Union Congress is, at best, one of co-ordination. Business representation was equally fragmented. In addition, producer interests have long had to vie with powerful financial interests. The latter, not needing a domestic base, have never enjoyed the close relationship with industry that its counterparts have elsewhere in Europe, and its ideology has always been profoundly non-interventionist.

The specific form of the institutions and practices associated with these two countries and the seven others included in this study are described in the next four sections of the current chapter. A very general description of the Austrian system of policy formulation, however, can be given in terms of the presence of:

- a network of institutions, including voluntary representative institutions and obligatory chambers, parity commissions, a national bank with social partners as board members, as well as all the elements of parliamentary democracy;
- a set of procedures, including the right of the social partners through institutions to comment upon legislative proposals, summit meetings to discuss macroeconomic parameters, and informal meetings; and
- the existence of consensus about the broad concerns of economic policy, namely that it should encourage growth and thereby hold down unemployment, rather than alter substantially the share of profits relative to that of wages.

By contrast, the UK system is structured around:

- primacy of government in the policymaking process with a high degree of initiative in the hands of the prime minister and leading cabinet ministers, and an exclusion of interest groups from the policy formulation process and their being consulted only as and when the government finds it appropriate or expedient;
- the absence of, abolition of, or relative unimportance of parity bodies with executive responsibilities;
- diverse opinions, across political parties and interest groups, concerning the goals of social and economic policy; and
- a suspicion, based upon experience, of arrangements that imply corporatism.

Moreover, it is also necessary to understand that in Austria there exists:

- a high degree of overlap between institutions, such that the positions of voluntary and obligatory associations and the positions of major political parties and organisations representing business and employees are closely co-ordinated; and
- a high degree of overlap in the functions exercised by a given individual, so that leading politicians and bankers currently occupy, or have occupied, significant office in a social partnership organisation.

By contrast, in the UK

- organisations and institutions are functionally specialised and concentrate on more narrowly defined tasks; and
- while there are cases of movement from office in an interest group to parliament and government, this generally implies in effect a formal break with the interest group.

2.2   MACROECONOMIC POLICY

The role of representative organisations of business and employees in macroeconomic policy making inevitably tends to be closely tied to their role in the management of wages and prices. In the 1960s, wages and prices policy came in many OECD countries to be seen as offering a 'third way' between Keynesian demand management policies, the inflationary implications of which were becoming apparent, and monetary policy, which was regarded as alien and brutal. Some policy makers believed that wages and prices policy meant more than just a way of shifting a country's position on the 'Phillips curve' to one associated with a lower level of unemployment. This was because they recognised such a policy as merely one element in economic and social policymaking that involved consensus on a broad range of long-term issues and on the way economic, social and political life was organised.

Table 2.1 Social partnership/dialogue and macroeconomic policy formulation

	Consensus	Institutions	Origins/history	Responsibilities	Policy making
Austria	Commitment to growth-oriented 'social market economy'	a. Formal and continuous (PKLP, ÖNB) b. Informal and continuous ('summit, of social partners', other meetings)	Long-standing	a. Reviewing, advising, vetting, drafting policy b. Reviewing, exchanging views, transferring information	Parliament and social partnership institutions
Germany	Acceptance of broad parameters of 'social market economy'	a. Informal and ad hoc b. 'Alliance for Jobs'	a. Long-standing b. Set up 1998	Exchanging views	Parliament
Netherlands	Acceptance of broad parameters of 'social market economy'	a. Formal but ad hoc (SER) b. Informal but regular (biannual exchanges) (STAR)	Long-standing	a. Advisory b. Reviewing, exchanging views, transferring information	Parliament
Sweden	Acceptance of broad parameters of 'social market economy'	Informal and ad hoc	Long-standing	Exchanging views	Parliament
France	Limited	a. Formal and regular (CES, CCN, CGdP) b. Ad hoc (summits)	Long-standing	a. Advising, transferring information b. Exchanging views	President/ Parliament

Country		Institutional form	Period	Functions	Policy-making
Italy	Limited	a. Formal but both regular and ad hoc meetings (CNEL) b. Informal but regulated by inter-sectoral agreement (biannual) and framework pacts	a. Set up under 1948 Constitution b. Since early 1990s	a. Advising, exchanging views b. Exchanging views, transferring information, limited drafting of policy in employment and social security matters	Parliament, with limited input of social partnership institutions
Spain	Limited	a. Formal (CES); informal (MI) b. Informal but regulated by inter-sectoral agreements	a. Since early 1990s b. Mid-1980s only	a. Advising, exchanging views b. Limited drafting of policy in social security matters	Parliament, with limited input of social partnership institutions
Ireland	Limited	a. Formal but ad hoc (NESC, NESF) b. Informal but regulated by inter-sectoral agreements ('Social Partnership')	a. Long-standing with new additions b. Since late 1980s	a. Advising, exchanging views, transferring information b. Reviewing, advising, vetting, drafting policy	Parliament and social partnership institutions
UK	Limited	a. Formal and regular (NEDC) b. Informal and ad hoc	a. Abolished 1992 b. Abandoned 1970s	Advising, exchanging views	Parliament

A Comparison of Structures

Austria stands out amongst all the countries covered in this book as having maintained such a consensus throughout the postwar period. For this reason, the involvement of the representatives of business in macroeconomic policy formulation in other EU member countries can best be understood by making a comparison with the extent to which the Austrian model is replicated elsewhere. The various countries may be categorised according to:

- the nature of the political consensus;
- the nature of the institutions in which social partners can participate;
- the history of these institutional arrangements;
- the tasks with which the institutions are charged and the responsibilities they have; and
- the locus of policy making – in other words, where decisions about policy are finally made.

These aspects are illustrated in Table 2.1, which distinguishes between various kinds of arrangement. First, there are institutions that are formally constituted in private or public law – decision-making bodies, such as the Austrian Parity Commission for Wages and Prices (PKLP), and consultative bodies, such as the French Economic and Social Council (CES). In contrast to these are arrangements that have a less formal basis. These include arrangements regulated by collective agreement, such as the Irish Social Partnership system and those which ensure regular review and information exchange, such as the bi-annual meetings between the Dutch government and the industry associations and unions organised together in the Foundation of Labour (STAR). In Spain, the Economic and Social Council (CES) was formally established in 1992, but the work of the Industry Round Table (Mesa de Industria) takes place in tripartite task groups. Second, Table 2.1 also distinguishes between procedures which involve regular contact, such as those which currently take place in Italy as the government plans its economic policy programme, and those which are convened to deal with a specific problem, such as the 1997 German Chancellor Round on Employment and Competitiveness.

Not included as advisory/consultative arrangements in Table 2.1 are simple, unsolicited representations. In all countries, associations of business and labour prepare, with varying degrees of precision, their own economic and political programmes and seek to propagate them. In all countries, too, such associations respond to particular policy initiatives announced by governments and call for policy action to deal with particular events or situations as they arise or as they become apparent. Equally, the fact that social partnership institutions are not involved in any formal or continuous way in macroeconomic policy making does not mean that the government of the country concerned gives only limited priority to the enhancement of state-provided social welfare or 'full employment'. For example, in **Sweden**, the trade unions consciously ceded responsibility for macroeconomic policy-making in the 1930s to the political arm of the labour movement (the Social Democratic Party). This was because they decided that the Social Democratic Party's control of parliament provided the best route to the achievement of their medium-term welfare objectives. This did not necessarily mean that the unions abandoned socialist objectives but simply that, instead of 'waiting for the inevitable collapse of capitalism', they would adopt a set of 'feasible policies' which, by generating full employment, would demonstrate the merits of their case (Korpi, 1978; see also Vartiainen, 1998).

In the case of **Austria**, critical actors were faced with the task of rebuilding a society that had been shattered politically and economically after the war. They therefore constructed a set of procedures and institutions that gave recognition to the interrelationships between taxation and expenditure policy, interest rate and exchange rate policy, industrial assistance and training policy, and social security and health and education policy. Wages policy, and accompanying it, prices policy, might have been part of a complex jigsaw puzzle, and the 'picture' would not have been complete without it, but equally that picture would not have been complete if the other parts had not fitted neatly together. Moreover, the act of fitting the parts together, and subsequently of keeping them together, was made possible only because those who were responsible for any one part were simultaneously responsible for the other parts too. This meant that they had the picture as a whole in their heads, the nature of their own contribution to it and the ability to recognise the parts that were contiguous and the way in which the matching should occur.

Table 2.1 underlines the distinctive nature of the Austrian case, even amongst those countries categorised as 'neo-corporatist'. At the opposite end of any spectrum of involvement is the **United Kingdom**, where the policy of the government since the start of the 1980s has been a rejection of 'demand-management' and with this of 'corporate capitalism' (Graham, 1997). In the eyes of many commentators, the performance of the UK economy over the postwar period was a testament to the inadequacies, even bankruptcy, of such corporate capitalism – even if it was an approach which, at the time, had been supported by associations representing both business and labour. Indeed, certain economic historians have pointed out how not only unions supported the corporatist approach because it provided a step towards their objective of a planned economy, but so too did industry associations since it offered the potential of greater stability (Fishbein, 1984).

Henceforth, prominence was given to monetary targets, markets and the individual. The third way of incomes policy, which had been an explicit component of government policy since the 1960s, and which had culminated in the mid-1970s in an attempt to establish a 'Social Contract' that tied wages policy to prices policy, personal tax policy and social expenditure policy, was rejected. Trade unions, in particular, were excluded from the policymaking process and by 1992 the sole forum where business, labour and government met to exchange views and to attempt the development of common solutions (the National Economic Development Council) had also been abolished. The new government elected in 1997 left the approach of the previous 18 years fundamentally unaltered, though it acted quickly to introduce a national minimum wage and mechanisms for statutory trade union recognition.

The Irish Experience

Between the two extremes of continuous involvement in the detail of policy making and exclusion fall the majority of EU member countries. Explicit participation in the policy drafting process is rare and limited. There have been cases of it in **Spain** and **Italy** where social pacts have been used to deal with highly specific subjects, such as employment security, training and pensions. However, although they formed critical elements in attempts to control public finances and increase employment opportunities, they are dealt with in the chapters on pay determination and employee relations, training and social security, rather than under the heading of macroeconomic policy. More ambitious in scope have been the social pacts in **Ireland** over the past decade, which use the title 'Social Partnership' and cover not only wages but also taxation, social welfare, education and health.

The antecedents of the 1987 'Social Partnership' project lie in the two National Understandings of 1978 and 1979, although a change of government led to the next eight years being characterised by a much more supply-side orientation and the responsibility for policy formation being held solely by parliament. However, a new government, prompted by the catastrophic situation in which Ireland then found itself – with high levels of inflation and unemployment, serious trade deficits and a large government deficit – prompted a second attempt to involve organisations representing business and employees in the search for a solution. Subsequently agreements have been drawn up at three-yearly intervals under the titles of Programme for National Recovery (1987–1990), Programme for Economic and Social Progress (1991–93), Programme for Competitiveness and Work (1994–96) and, currently, Partnership 2000 for Inclusion, Employment and Competitiveness (1997–2001).

There is little doubt that the Irish experiment was influenced by the British experiments of the mid-1970s, when the UK government had tried to make income tax cuts contingent upon adherence to the terms of its wages policy under the Social Contract. The government and trade unions had then talked of the need to increase social expenditure and made reference to a 'social wage' (Fishbein, 1984). However, the Irish measures went much further and were much more formal. They have been predicated upon 'agreement(s) on pay and conditions' reached between the peak organisations of employers and workers which are developed into wider documents of understanding through discussion with a range of interest groups. In preambles, agreement is expressed on the need for policies which restrain public spending, maintain a firm exchange rate strategy, enhance competitiveness and strengthen economic and social solidarity. Specific elements include tax cuts in return for wage restraint, such that in the current agreement direct tax reductions will provide some one-third of the envisaged increase in take-home pay. Other elements include action programmes covering the maintenance or expansion of the social welfare system, the promotion of enterprise, jobs and business formation, co-determination at the workplace and individual and collective rights and the reduction of poverty.

The Irish social partnership agreements are merely statements of common understanding and intent. They have no status beyond that accorded them by the parties that attended the talks or signed the agreements and require ratification by each of the unions affiliated to the Irish Congress of Trade Unions. However, at the same time they are not only the product of discussion and submissions by interested organisations and groupings, but also build upon advisory reports drawn up by a tripartite advisory council whose members are reinforced by government-appointed external experts. Indeed, since 1993 a supplementary body – the National Economic and Social Forum – has also been set up representing a still wider spread of social groups including the churches, the unemployed, young people and women, small business and even the main political parties. Moreover, progress on attaining the objectives of the agreements is monitored on a regular basis by a specially constituted committee of the parties to the agreement. Accordingly, it can be said that there are certain close parallels between practices and structures in Ireland and Austria, with the principal difference being the relative novelty of those in the former country.

Experiences of Other European Countries

Elsewhere, it is through participation in advisory, liaison or consultative meetings rather than participation in 'rule-' or 'policymaking' bodies that business and employee groups are formally involved in macroeconomic policy formation. Such participation can be in a forum, which has been constituted in public law, or in one that has developed through custom and practice and has no statutory footing. Equally, participation can be on a regular basis or on an ad hoc basis, at meetings to deal with a specific subject. Referring back to Table 2.1, it can be seen that almost all permutations are possible.

Statutory bodies may be charged with a reactive and/or a proactive role. They can comment on proposals submitted by government or, if meeting on a regular basis, will usually have the power to initiate their own reports or 'opinions'. Regular bodies are normally drawn in at a particular stage in the policymaking process, for instance at the time when budgets are being prepared. Ad hoc bodies respond to a particular situation, often when governments are seeking to explore solutions to highly sensitive subjects and where legitimacy is sought by the involvement of the principal actors affected.

Countries pursue a wide gamut of approaches. Thus, the influence of the Economic and Social Council in France is limited, despite its place being established in the constitution. At critical points, the French government may therefore convene alternatives, such as the joint declaration signed by all social partners in February 1995 on a variety of labour market issues and the tripartite national conference on employment, pay and working time held in October 1997. Nor, by their very nature, do governments have any obligations to respect the views contained in 'opinions' which advisory bodies may issue or the views they may express at meetings. Only when the body has been granted a cornerstone role in policy making, as has the Foundation of Labour in the Netherlands, must its contribution be taken into account, whether or not the body or the meeting has any formal status. It is noteworthy that the Social-Economic Council (SER) - a tripartite body with government appointed experts plus the unions and employers - which was set up under public law with a statutory right of consultation on all matters of law/policy making in the social/economic sphere, currently has a less pivotal role than the Foundation of Labour. Its statutory right of consultation was removed in 1995, at least partly because it had been unable to give unanimous advice about anything - except on the Maastricht convergence criteria in 1992 - over the last decades.[1]

Cycles of Involvement

With the exception of Austria, where social partnership has been integral to macroeconomic policy formation throughout the postwar period, the involvement of business and employee interest groups in anything more than a consultative role has occurred at best in cycles and often only spasmodically. As has already been made clear, in the 1960s and 1970s, the UK appeared to be a strongly neo-corporatist country.

Germany, too, was studied for its efforts at 'Concerted Action' over the decade 1967-77. The German economic framework is based on a subtle system of checks and balances between the various institutions governing areas like corporate governance, collective bargaining and banking, allied to a widely-shared consensus on the importance of export competitiveness (Streeck, 1992a; Charkham, 1994). However, over the 1967-77 period, a social democratic government, initially committed to Keynesian economics, offered employers and, more particularly, trade unions further opportunities to participate in economic and social policy making in return for wage bargaining respecting the need to minimise inflation. The experiment foundered for a number of reasons. One was that the unions believed that it was too concerned with wages relative to prices, and another was the failure of the government to deliver meaningful involvement on broader issues, or even to legislate for the extensions of enterprise and workplace co-determination that they had sought (Clark, 1979).

It was not for a further 20 years, when unemployment was reaching levels not seen since the 1930s, that a functional equivalent of Concerted Action was resurrected. The trade unions proposed an 'Alliance for Jobs' which focused on government action on employment, unemployment, training, flexibility and social security in return for wage moderation. However, the enthusiasm of the government and of business associations was at best limited. A tripartite summit (Chancellor Round) in 1996 resulted in an Alliance for Jobs and Competitiveness which was much more general than the original proposal and, although it committed the parties to attempting to halve unemployment by the end of the decade, said little about social security. Very shortly afterwards, the government unilaterally adopted a 50-point 'action programme' which was heavily supply-side oriented, aiming to reduce the size of the public sector and public expenditure, cut back on taxes and social security and deregulate the labour market. Despite this disappointment, the unions renewed their proposal for an Alliance for Jobs two years later and were this time rewarded when a Social Democrat-led 'red-green' government was formed shortly after the general elections in September 1998. The government and the social partners agreed the following December to establish an Alliance for Jobs (Bündnis für Arbeit) which took the form of a permanent tripartite body. According to the 'joint declaration of the alliance for jobs, vocational training and competitiveness' that followed, the parties resolved to carry out a series of measures including a reduction of non-wage labour costs, reforms of the country's social security and company taxation systems and greater opportunities for small- and medium-sized enterprises to obtain risk capital (EIRO, DE9812286N).

A rather less ambitious, and in essence much more piecemeal or incremental, approach has been followed in the **Netherlands**. In the 1950s and early 1960s, the Netherlands, too, was described as a corporatist society, and macroeconomic policy was built primarily around negotiated wage restraint. The consensus for this collapsed by the mid 1960s and attempts to restore it had to wait until the impact of the second oil shock – manifesting itself in rapidly rising unemployment and, by Dutch standards, high inflation (Visser, 1991). The government threatened to impose a wages and prices freeze, and to avoid this, and to protect their area of influence in this domain, unions and employers reached the first of a series of 'accords' covering pay and employment (Visser, 1998). However, when doing so, they also effectively acknowledged the prerogative of the government to manage and control public finances, including where these had implications for the social security system (see section below on social security). A cornerstone of the Dutch accords has subsequently been the biannual meetings between business associations, unions and government, once to discuss the basis of the budget and budget plans and once at the start of the wage round, to ensure that both sides are aware of each other's intentions. Such meetings are designed to guarantee that employers and unions can make an assessment of the tax and social contributions that might be levied, and so of net pay, and in this respect there are similarities with what occurs in Ireland under the social partnership arrangements there. They are also designed to ensure that the implications of settlements for certain social minimum benefits are clear, since these benefits are normally adjusted in line with wages and might be de-coupled from them if wages grow too fast.

Prospects

Involving social partners in macroeconomic policy formulation is a fraught process and not surprisingly relatively unusual. Arrangements are subject to criticism in many countries because they imply non-elected and/or not necessarily fully representative groups participating in what is commonly regarded as the prerogative of governments and parliaments. Involving them also means that organisations find themselves cast in a role that they may feel is inappropriate to their objectives. In particular, there tends to be criticism within some sections of the union movements in many countries about whether or not their role is one of economic management (for Germany, see Clark, 1979). Or they may feel obliged to consent to programmes about which they have doubts – an example being the way in which the unions in Austria had to accept substantial public expenditure retrenchments in the 1990s that were designed to help meet Maastricht convergence criteria (Falkner, 1996; Guger, 1998).

This is not to suggest that structures in Austria are precarious, but it does imply a certain fragility in arrangements elsewhere. Table 2.2 illustrates what this means.

Table 2.2   Potential strains on social partner involvement in macroeconomic policy formulation

Country	Time	Issue
Austria	Mid-1990s	Budget consolidation to meet EMU convergence criteria
Germany	Now	Operation of Alliance for Jobs and regional pacts
Netherlands	1980s	Government given free hand to deal with public expenditure
Sweden		Not applicable (social partners have historically accepted that governments are responsible for macroeconomic policy)
France	Now	Failure to carry employers at 1997 employment summit
Italy	Now	Implementation of details of 1996 Pact for Employment and operation of territorial and regional pacts
Spain	Mid-1980s	Failure of 1985–86 economic and social accord and operation of regional pacts
Ireland	Now	Criticisms from certain trade unions, sustainability of tax cuts given EMU convergence criteria
UK		Not applicable (but note certain trade union frustration with new Labour government)

The case of Germany has already been referred to. Mention should also be made to **Spain.** Since the restoration of democracy, more or less formal pacts had been agreed covering pay on various occasions. In 1995 an attempt to extend such pacts to cover social security issues failed when the unions saw the government as failing to deliver and acting unilaterally on pension reform (Recio and Roca, 1998). Thereafter, intersectoral agreements have been limited to highly specific aspects of employee relations (see section below on pay determination and employee relations). One-off efforts to mobilise support are likely to be particularly fraught if there is no basis for working together or for shared understanding of problems and solutions.

In **Italy** a further intersectoral agreement was concluded in 1996, known as the Pact for Employment, which formed the basis for a framework law in 1997. This set out the government's programme on a range of issues relating to labour market flexibility, temporary work, youth unemployment and aid for small enterprises and for the poor regions of the south (Regalia and Regini, 1998; Negrelli and Treu, 1999).

With respect to 'problems', an understanding of where the economy stands and is likely to go is important. The participants in social partnership arrangements and experiments in Austria, the Netherlands and Ireland can in each case call on the resources of an officially recognised, respected and independent forecasting body. In Austria this is the Institute for Economic Research (WIFO); in the Netherlands it is the Central Planning Bureau (CPB); and in Ireland it is the Economic and Social Research Institute (ESRI). In Germany, by contrast, during the Concerted Action period, much energy was spent on discussing the validity of the government's models and the assumptions that were being fed into them. Germany has a number of major economic forecasting institutes, and these by no means always agree with one another. At least in many of the larger European countries, where there is also a plethora of forecasters and forecasts, it is difficult to build the basis of agreement, since plausible, 'scientific' alternatives can nearly always be offered.

With respect to 'solutions', the recent case of **France** is worthy of consideration. As noted above, the social partners were invited to an employment summit in October 1997 that discussed job creation, especially for young people, early retirement and social security reform. However, the employers' organisations were fundamentally opposed to the government's core project of cutting working time. They walked away from the discussion leaving the government to respond by introducing legislation for which it could not claim bipartisan support. The statutory 35-hour week was subsequently enacted in June 1998. Employers in Italy similarly refused to contemplate the inclusion of a general working time reduction in the 1996 Pact for Employment and so also limited the extent to which it dealt with broader issues of occupational training.

Even the Irish experiment in social partnership has not run entirely without problems. Trade unions in the high-productivity exporting sectors have felt that they have been disadvantaged by adherence to central agreements to restrain pay. However, in 1998, it has also been public sector workers who have been pushing for 'a more generous interpretation' of the pay guidelines (*Financial Times*, 21 July 1998). More critical to the sustainability of the agreements reached is the ability of the government to meet commitments to ensure that take-home pay increases even if gross pay is restrained. With the economy growing (if anything) over fast, and with public expenditure already high, the government is being urged to avoid 'overheating' as the launch of the single currency approaches. The interest rate tool that a government can use to effect a 'cooling down' of an economy is no longer available to the Irish government, since the country is already in the embryonic single currency system. This means that much more of the burden falls on fiscal policy. If the government has to tighten this, the scope it has for granting the tax cuts to which it is committed, or to which it might wish to commit itself in the future, is limited, even if the public sector unions can be held 'in line'. Others who wish to emulate experiments in trading wage restraint off against taxes – an explicit component of the Irish experiment and implicit in the Dutch one – will no doubt have to be aware of the delicate balance that such an approach has to achieve, and of the increasingly limited room in which the relevant actors have to manoeuvre.

2.3   PAY DETERMINATION AND EMPLOYEE RELATIONS

Pay determination and employee relations are the traditional subject matter of joint regulation by employers and unions. Pay includes the settlement of minimum and basic rates of pay, pay structures and the principles and levels of pay increases. Employee relations include the regulation of terms other than pay, especially working time, the form of the employment contract and the procedural frameworks that govern the conduct of the social partners.

The struggle by unions for recognition, employers' responses and the role of the state in moulding industrial relations systems through legislation have led to a variety of institutional, legal and social frameworks that characterise the current European patchwork of labour relations. In some countries, such as Austria, France and Germany, the role of legal regulation is central. In others, notably the Nordic countries, collective agreements at central level determine the nature of industrial relations, while in a third group – Ireland and the UK – a voluntarist system broadly predominates. Here employers and unions are left to negotiate their own relationships, with the state generally playing a minimal role.

Centralised Bargaining

One of the most striking aspects of industrial relations across Europe is the difference between countries with respect to the level at which issues of pay and employment conditions are determined. Table 2.3 presents a summary in terms both of the subject matter of joint determination and whether agreements are made at the national, sectoral or company and workplace level. This section starts with a description of the role of centralised negotiations. Austria provides a classic example of this. The UK is, and always has been, at the very opposite end of the spectrum. Even when industry-level agreements were more common, these were frequently topped up by local level agreements and served at best to fix certain minima. The section also shows that, as well as setting broad parameters for wages, in some European countries national agreements can be used to regulate the use of certain kinds of labour, to settle certain basic parameters of the employment relationship and to bring clarity into industrial relations structures.

In **Austria**, the wage negotiation process opens in the Subcommittee on Wages of the Parity Commission for Wages and Prices. This means that the social partners at peak level can determine the timing of negotiations, which gives them the chance to dampen cost-push inflation by postponing negotiations and to ensure that unions' various pay claims across sectors are in line with macroeconomic and employment realities. Pay negotiations open with the metalworking sector, the most densely unionised, which acts as leader. Claims are oriented in line with average national labour productivity. ´Additional settlements at plant level may set rates above (but not below) those established at sector level. Austria has been frequently noted for its high degree of aggregate real wage flexibility, and this is attributed to the concern of those negotiating wages with movements in economy-wide productivity and

Table 2.3 *Bargaining levels in selected countries*

Country	Pay	Working time	Employment security
European Union	N/A	1993 Working Time Directive	Series of Directives (atypical work etc.)
Austria	Centralised with metal industry as wage leader; workplace agreements now permitted	Sector-level agreements; workplace agreements now permitted	Sector-level bargaining
Sweden	Decentralisation to sector and company level	Working time not an issue	Detail co-determined at company level
Germany	Degree of sectoral co-ordination; regional dimension; decentralisation to works councils	Negotiations at sector level; decentralisation to workplace levels	Detail co-determined at company level
Netherlands	Decentralisation to sector and company levels	Law allows negotiation of flexibility; sector and company level agreements	Detail co-determined at company level
France	Requirement to bargain collectively – expansion at all levels; decentralisation to trade union delegates	Law on 35-hour week introduced following failure to agree at national level; details negotiated at 'lowest' levels	Detail negotiated at company level
Italy	Rationalisation of structures through social pacts; regional dimension	Law allows negotiation of flexibility at sector and company level	Social pact regulates part-time and temporary work etc.
Spain	Rationalisation of structures through social pacts; regional dimension	Law allows negotiation of flexibility at sector and company levels	Social pact regulates new forms of work contract
UK	Decentralisation to company and workplace levels	Company level agreements (or unilateral imposition)	Company level agreements (or unilateral imposition)
Ireland	Central agreements on overall limits followed by other sectors	National pay agreement (1988–90) introduced 39-hour week; details negotiated at company level	National agreements; company-level negotiation

with the country's relative competitiveness. Sector-level agreements cover issues like working conditions, health and safety and working time, and may be extended to cover all workers, both unionised and non-unionised.

Centralised wage fixing is effectively an on-going process in Austria. For more than ten years, this has also been the case in **Ireland**. There, a form of national bargaining – known as Social Partnership – has, since 1987, produced a series of three-yearly programmes covering pay increases and many other issues of economic and social policy. The agreement on pay in partnership programmes appears as bipartite but the government is closely involved. Wage restraint is traded off for a commitment by the government to reduce direct taxation and to follow a broadly agreed programme of maintaining and expanding public services and investment in infrastructural and human capital. These aspects have been detailed in the previous section. Pay agreements under Social Partnership cover the whole country apart from the public service (and construction on two occasions). For the most part, local bargaining is ruled out by these agreements which have prevented wage drift. It is widely agreed that wage restraint has contributed to Irish economic performance over recent years.

In other European countries, central agreements on pay have been more ad hoc. After the restoration of democracy in **Spain** there were a number of national agreements between employers and unions which laid down pay guidelines, but by the mid-1980s consensus had evaporated. In the **Netherlands**, however, an agreement between the central organisations of business and labour negotiated in 1982 – the so-called Wassenaar Agreement – is commonly viewed as providing the starting-point for that country's subsequent recovery. It was reached if only to pre-empt a government-imposed freeze on wages and prices and direct government intervention in the bargaining process. It suspended the established principle of including a cost-of-living adjustment clause in wage settlements.

As a trade-off, employers lifted their outright refusal to discuss reductions in working time, while both sides accepted the need for settlements to concentrate on improving employment opportunities rather than simply increasing pay. In 1989, a second tripartite agreement sought to stress this principle, although compliance with it was by no means always complete. Indeed, government intervention was threatened again in the early 1990s. This prompted the third major agreement, the so-called New Course Agreement in 1993 – though this one was bipartite – which again contained a trade-off on working time. It formally recognised that 'all proposals ... should be tested for their possible effects on and their contribution to the reinforcement of the profitability and competitiveness of companies, as well as their increase in labour participation and employment' (Foundation of Labour, 1993).

Tripartite intersectoral agreements, designed to curb labour costs, had been signed in **Italy** in 1983 and 1984 (Negrelli and Santi, 1991), but no further activity took place at this level until the 1990s. It was not until the early 1990s, when the country faced the need to meet the Maastricht criteria for entry into European Monetary Union and the main political parties had collapsed in scandal, that a technocratic government sought to initiate wide-ranging reforms of the labour market. The first in a series of tripartite agreements was signed in 1992. Despite much resistance from the union side, this abolished the country's pay indexation system which had linked wage levels to prices since shortly after the end of the Second World War. The 1992 pact was followed by a second the following year that sought to reform the collective bargaining system and by the Pact for Employment in 1996, as noted above.

As well as providing examples of potentially influential one-off agreements or pacts, the Netherlands and Italy share another feature in common. The wage negotiation process in both countries is influenced by biannual meetings between government and the social partners. At these, expectations and projected outcomes are discussed. In the Netherlands, these meetings have no formal status, but rely on custom and practice; in Italy, they are specified in the terms of the 1993 intersectoral agreement.

National or intersectoral agreements have also been used to settle the circumstances in which various forms of non-standard labour – particularly part-time and temporary workers – can be used and the entitlements that non-standard workers have. Thus, the regulation of atypical work was the subject of such an agreement in **France** in 1990, while the 1996 Pact for Employment in **Italy**, which contained clauses on temporary work and flexible working time, required employers to contribute 5 per cent of the relevant wage costs towards training provision when hiring temporary staff. A remarkable proliferation of fixed-term contract working occurred in **Spain** in the 1980s and 1990s, as employers sought to evade restrictions on declaring redundancies and the high compensation payments that had to be made to the workers affected. By the early 1990s, Spain had one of the highest levels of temporary working in Europe and almost all new recruitment was being made on the basis of fixed-term contracts. In 1994 the government had tried to act unilaterally to introduce labour reforms, including legislation to make it easier for employers to make redundancies, but one of the responses to this was a general strike. By contrast, in 1997, job security and measures to boost employment were the subject of one of a set of three intersectoral agreements – the so-called April Accords. The most notable innovation was a new contract aimed at groups of workers finding it difficult to gain a foothold in the labour market (the long-term unemployed, young people and people with disabilities, amongst others). This traded off open-ended (that is, secure) employment with reduced levels of severance pay in case of redundancy.

In the Agreement of Haarlem, also known as the Agreement on Flexibility and Security, of 1996, the social partners in the **Netherlands** had sought to tie regulation of the use of temporary workers, and an enhancement of such workers' rights, into an easing of restrictions on redundancy. These aspects of the Haarlem Agreement were presented to the government on a 'take it or leave it' basis, and they were enacted as such into labour legislation.

Tripartite and bipartite intersectoral negotiation has been used in a number of countries not only to settle issues of pay or employment conditions but also to encourage reform of the industrial relations system itself. Both **Italy** and **Spain** had, over the decades, seen the development of structures that were now recognised as complex, fragmented, unwieldy and characterised by an excessive overlap between the competences of actors at the level of sector, company, workplace and region. In Italy, the tripartite agreement of 1993 sought to bring more order into the structure of collective bargaining. Under its terms, negotiations at sector level covering procedural and normative matters take place every four years while those covering pay take place every two. In addition, four-yearly agreements may also be negotiated at a 'decentralised' level – which might mean company or region – to cover other issues not dealt with by the sector. The agreement also reformed trade union representation at establishment level. Similarly in Spain, one of the 1997 April Accords sought to streamline collective bargaining by laying out measures to co-ordinate the different levels at which negotiations could take place and give greater scope to local level bargaining on pay structures (Martín Valverde, 1999).

The 1990 Industrial Relations Act sought to foster and encourage collective bargaining at enterprise level in **Ireland**. The national framework for the conduct of industrial relations and the resolution of disputes that it provides was incorporated into the Social Partnership programme. Under the present programme, the social partners have subscribed to a National Framework for Partnership for Competitive Enterprises, which seeks ways to establish partnership at enterprise level, and a National Centre for Partnership was set up in 1997 to promote training in partnership skills at enterprise level. Equally, in the **Netherlands**, a series of framework agreements reached by the Foundation of Labour in the 1990s recognised the requirement to decentralise. As in Germany, law had tightly circumscribed the competence of works councils. However, in reality there had been a series of enterprise level agreements covering issues like reorganisation and mergers. The 1993 New Course Agreement placed a seal of approval on these developments by stressing the significance of local negotiations in ensuring profitability and competitiveness of companies.

Decentralisation of Bargaining

In recent years, the social partners have concentrated increasingly on supply-side factors in promoting competitiveness at all levels in the economy. Accordingly, while intersectoral agreements have a role to play, the fact that these have also been used to reform collective bargaining structures bears testimony to a recognition that in many ways negotiations have to be brought closer to the workplace. Thus, in all the countries studied there have been trends towards negotiating pay and employment conditions at levels lower than that of the industrial sector – either at that of the company or at that of the individual workplace – in an attempt to ensure that they more exactly match the cost and productivity requirements of individual companies and workplaces. Reductions in working time have often also accompanied its reorganisation into more flexible patterns to improve utilisation of existing levels of capital and labour.

Decentralisation, whether in unregulated or regulated form, is a major theme in pay determination. In the case of the **United Kingdom**, for instance, sector-level bargaining has fragmented over the past 15 years or so and pay in the private sector is settled principally at company or workplace level, often through performance appraisal or performance-related pay systems and without any joint regulation at all.

However, decentralisation, in a more or less regulated fashion, has also taken place elsewhere in Europe. A notable example of this is what has occurred in **Sweden**. Pay negotiations there now take place at sectoral level and at company, and even workplace, level. The third level – the intersectoral or multi-industry level, which had been such a significant feature of the Swedish model since the 1950s – has now vanished, and with it the associated notion of solidaristic pay policy. The principal employers' organisation (SAF) abandoned intersectoral bargaining in 1990 because of inflationary pressures. The government intervened by appointing a tripartite national mediation commission (the Rehnberg Commission) which reached a two-year stabilisation agreement for the entire economy for 1991–93, subsequently renewed for 1993–95. This brief period reflected a new kind of centralised bargaining with an active role for the state, but very little local bargaining. However, the Commission lapsed in 1995, and the current two-tier system was consolidated. It had been evolving over the 1980s, as the contents of intersectoral agreements became less and less detailed and their provisions were increasingly superseded by sectoral and local negotiations. This process of decentralisation was accompanied by the introduction of new kinds of pay systems and profit-sharing schemes. It was also accompanied by local level deviation from sectoral agreements. Enterprises unable to pay a negotiated increase can, and do, defer all or part of it, if they gain the agreement of the local trade union. Lastly, decentralisation was also accompanied by a greater flexibility in working time practices. Sectoral agreements set broad parameters, but it is at the local level that unions and management can come to agreement to set working time patterns appropriate to the needs of the particular workplace.

German labour legislation has attempted to prevent competition between the works councils and the unions by reserving collective bargaining and the right to call strikes to the unions alone. Collective bargaining in **Germany** was primarily at the sectoral level. As in the case of the solidaristic wages policy in Sweden, such a relatively centralised system was promoted as having a positive impact on productivity, in that both provided a way of driving out marginal units of production. However, in recent years, the distinction between sector-level negotiations and company/workplace-level negotiations, and hence the relative competences of unions and works councils, has become blurred. This can be attributed in part to the requirement to manage the most efficient introduction of collectively agreed general reductions in working time – a principle first set out in the Lederer Compromise of 1984 that settled the metal industry strike for an across-the-board cut in hours. In part, too, the blurring has been a response to the need to save jobs and indeed whole workplaces or enterprises by keeping down labour costs and introducing new working practices. In this context, there has been an increasing number of works agreements that have infringed the minimum conditions laid down by sector-level agreement in exchange for the maintenance of employment levels.

These developments have led to agonised debate about whether or not the 'German model' still exists. The German industry associations favour these developments, arguing that the 'basic consensus' about the value of sector-level negotiations and uniform levels of pay has broken down, while the employers' associations have been more willing to defend the system provided that greater differentiation be allowed to suit individual circumstances. The unions have found themselves in an ambivalent position, but their local representatives – who themselves are often also members of works councils – are the very same people who negotiate alternatives and options at workplace level. The 1997 agreement for the chemical industry, for example, now allows downward deviations in pay by up to 10 per cent 'especially where [the firm] is faced with economic difficulties'. Settlements granting employers unilateral rights to pay lower rates are, of course, strongly contested. German unions have, however, reluctantly accepted the insertion of 'opening clauses' into collective agreements to permit negotiated deviations in cases of firms in difficulty.

The process of decentralisation can provoke a challenge to the capacity of the industrial relations system. In **France**, successive governments have actively pursued a policy of decentralisation through the extension and consolidation of collective bargaining, particularly at company level, as a means to achieve greater flexibility in pay at the workplace. The Auroux law of 1982 required companies, where union workplace branches had been formed, to enter negotiations every year on pay, working hours and patterns of working time. However, because in the large majority of workplaces there is no union representation, the wished-for joint regulation was infrequent. Legislation in 1996 has permitted non-unionised staff to elect a representative to negotiate on their behalf and, failing that, a nationally recognised union to mandate an employee to bargain for it. The Aubry law on the 35-hour week, adopted in May 1998, builds on these innovations by requiring its details – covering matters like the extent of wage compensation and the adaptation of working time schedules – also to be negotiated at the lowest level possible. Leaving details of implementation to local negotiation grants, potentially, considerable opportunities to employers to reorganise their labour force and this has been recognised by some as at least partial compensation for the government's unilateral imposition of a cut in working time (*Financial Times*, 20 May 1998).

The absence of a local level bargaining capacity – on both management and union sides – has been offered as an explanation for the failure of attempts to decentralise bargaining in **Austria** (Reithofer, 1995). A number of the sectoral agreements concluded in 1993 contained 'opening clauses' allowing deferral of a small proportion of the negotiated increase by enterprises making additional investments that could be shown to increase or stabilise employment. There were few instances where this opportunity was used. In negotiations at national level between the social partners on a law that would give greater flexibility to working time patterns, the unions strongly resisted employer calls for the ability of settlements to be made at enterprise level, because they doubted the ability of works councils to counter management designs. Although the 1997 law relaxes previous restrictions, it recognises only those flexible working time patterns that are agreed at sector level.

Changing Dimensions of Partnership

Throughout much of the 1980s and 1990s, Conservative governments in the **United Kingdom** acted to reduce the role of any approximation of social partnership in management of the economy. In the area of pay and employee relations, this approach was pursued with greatest intensity. Laws designed to reduce the powers of trade unions to recruit members, organise or take strike action were enacted. Protective labour legislation was weakened and wages councils, which set minimum pay levels across certain sectors, were abolished. This is a clear example of decentralisation going hand in hand with, and indeed being a consequence of, attempts at deregulation.

However, decentralisation of industrial relations does not have to imply a reduction of the role of social partnership, as in some cases it may merely mean that key actors and concerns have changed. In the language of some commentators, for example, decentralisation may be associated with 'empowerment' – that is, the devolution of 'power and responsibilities to teams at workplace and customer level' (Beardwell and Holden, 1997: 643–4).

Indeed, commentators have sought to describe some of the processes discussed above in terms of 'centralised decentralisation' (Due et al., 1995) or 'organised decentralisation' (Traxler, 1995a). Both terms emphasise two parallel or co-existing trends. The first is that decision-making processes have been institutionalised at local levels in the organisation by ensuring access of the local parties involved to information and discretionary powers. The second is that centralised decision-making processes have been restructured at the same time, thereby allowing the central level to retain control of the decision-making processes, albeit through 'more indirect mechanisms' (Due et al., 1995: 121). In other words, decentralisation may co-exist with changing patterns of central control rather than act in opposition to them, as in a zero-sum model. Traxler, in distinguishing between 'organised' and 'disorganised' decentralisation, argues that 'attention should be paid not only to the level of bargaining, but also to the degree of its co-ordination' (1995a: 5).

Therefore, while the UK might present an example of disorganised decentralisation, the Netherlands and Ireland by contrast illustrate attempts at organised decentralisation. In **Germany,** however, developments are rather more ambiguous. There, a diminution of the role of partnership and dialogue with respect to pay and employee relations was a consequence less of deliberate action by agreement but rather of broader economic and political pressures. Collective agreements cover almost all industries but, unless they are extended by law, they do not necessarily cover all employers within the sector but only those who are members of the relevant employers' association. Already in the 1980s, industrial relations academics were pointing to enterprises and workplaces where there was no employee representative on the company supervisory board and where no works council operated. As much as 50 per cent of the workforce was estimated as being employed in these so-called 'white spaces'. More recently, yet higher estimates – 61 per cent in the 1990s – have been made (Bertelsmann Stiftung/

Hans-Böckler-Stiftung, 1998: 10). Works council penetration is also much lower in the new states of the east, where the newly privatised enterprises have also been disinclined to join employers' associations, and throughout the country, newly started up companies tend neither to have works councils nor to be members of an employers' association. In Germany, a form of disorganised decentralisation appears to be occurring.

It is possible that the same is occurring in **Austria**, too. As in Germany, the negotiation of wages is not within the competence of works councils. In practice, large companies have made settlements with their works councils, while small companies and sometimes whole subsectors have ignored the terms of collective agreements and paid their own, lower rates. The extent of such practices is difficult to determine and seldom admitted to publicly. A high variance in wages seems also matched by a high variance in other working conditions. An initial inquiry into the impact of the 1997 law on working time suggested that it might have had little effect on practice because flexible work patterns were already widespread. One industry representative was quoted as estimating that, in the past, 'unlawful' working practices could be found in between one-third and one-half of all establishments (EIRO, AT9702102F).

Prospects

Three issues arise out of this overview of trends in the role of social partnership/dialogue in the determination of pay and employee relations – decentralisation, rationalisation and trust. From a practical point of view, decentralisation is the most important and several points need to be made with respect to it.

The requirement for flexibility and adaptability acknowledged by governments and social partners at peak levels has created the need to perform new tasks at workplace level. The reorganisation of working patterns to ensure maximum capital utilisation time and the introduction of new production techniques and more flexible payment systems all require design, implementation, monitoring and assessment. Employers can, of course, carry out these tasks by themselves, using techniques of scientific management or human resource management. Or they can adapt and even promote frameworks of employee representation that stretch from the workplace level up to the boardroom to help them.

In many countries it is possible to talk of the development of 'supply-side corporatism'. That is, one of the evolving functions of the social partners is to focus attention on to the workplace and negotiate new forms of working. This includes improvements in work organisation, the introduction of appropriate technology, the acquisition of new skills and the adaptation of pay systems that will increase the productivity and profitability of the company and ensure long-term employment security.

The representational status of the social partners and their ability to enforce joint decisions can, of course, be underpinned by legislation, but it can also be underpinned by major collective agreements. Joint regulation ensures that 'flexibility' does not lead to chaotic deregulation and it protects workers against the excesses of 'efficiency' and 'competitiveness' through the local regulation of working time, non-standard contracts and redundancy. In the same way, joint regulation can be used to rationalise bargaining structures – as in Italy and Spain – and to create or maintain trust between the social partners.

Of all the countries covered in this book, decentralisation appears to pose the greatest challenge in **Austria** and **Germany**. This does not mean that there are no trends to decentralise in each of these countries, or that informally there is a much higher degree of decentralisation than is legally permitted or formally recognised. Rather, the problem is that legal and industrial relations frameworks need to adapt more systematically if decentralisation is to be handled in a genuinely 'organised' fashion. As made clear in Table 2.4, the social partners need to espouse greater decentralisation more wholeheartedly if they are to remain in control of the process.

Table 2.4   Issues in pay and employee relations

Austria	Recognition and control of decentralisation
Germany	Recognition and control of decentralisation
Netherlands	Consolidation of reform
Sweden	Consolidation of reform
France	Improving workplace representation structures
Italy	Rationalising bargaining structures, social pacts
Spain	Rationalising bargaining structures
Ireland	Ensuring stability/durability of new system
UK	Creation of trust

In **Sweden** and the **Netherlands,** by contrast, decentralisation is both occurring and apparently under control. In both these countries the relevant institutions are well established and appear relatively stable. No doubt there will still be disagreement about the direction to be taken, particularly in Sweden where employers advocate still further decentralisation of pay determination. However, both countries are otherwise characterised by a degree of confidence in their approach. In **Ireland,** too, the social partners are broadly confident, but the institutional structure upon which their tripartite system has developed is more recent than in the other two countries. For this reason, however comprehensive the Irish approach is, it still has an aura of precariousness about it.

Nevertheless, Ireland appears to have progressed further than **Italy** or **Spain.** In both these countries, the need to develop and rationalise appropriate negotiating structures at the local level is recognised, and the first steps have been taken though more has yet to be achieved. Without appropriate structures, neither the insights nor the expertise of the social partners that are needed to deal with the agenda of supply-side corporatism can be developed, or, where they do exist, they cannot be used to effect. This, ultimately, is the problem in **France,** too. Workplace representative structures exist on paper, but active involvement in workplace governance, particularly as mediated by trade unions, remains limited.

Lastly, the case of the **United Kingdom** demonstrates that the management of competitiveness needs to be founded on greater levels of trust between employers, unions and government. For many, the term social partnership is at best an alien term and at worst a synonym for inefficiency and failure. Yet it is noticeable that in recent years, particularly with the election of the Labour government in 1997, the term has reappeared in political discourse. Although the new government made clear that it intended to retain the industrial relations laws passed by its predecessors, it has also shown itself more willing to engage in dialogue with unions and business interests. In preparing legislation to introduce a minimum wage, it set up a Commission on Low Pay to investigate the details and to propose an appropriate hourly sum. Members of the Commission were drawn from a wide variety of organisations with an interest in the issue. To give them independence and room for discussion, they sat on the Commission not as representatives of organisations but as individuals, but their unanimous report was hailed by the government as an example of involvement and social partnership. Similarly, in describing the consultations around recent legislation on dismissal protection and union recognition, the government referred to its 'programme to replace the notion of conflict between employers and employees with the promotion of partnership' (Department of Trade and Industry, 1998: 1). Although the end result satisfied neither all unions nor all employers, the principal business association in the UK described the compromise achieved as a 'workable and sound basis' for the future conduct of industrial relations.

At company level, too, relations between certain employers and unions in the UK had already begun to take a new direction since the early 1990s with the conclusion of a growing number of job security agreements, which seemed to reflect a new mood of partnership (EIRO, UK9810153F). Job security agreements (JSAs) have been used to manage the process of change not only in private-sector manufacturing companies but also more recently in retail and financial services as well. Though limited in numbers and often negotiated during a period of crisis, JSAs guarantee jobs in exchange for introducing greater flexibility into working practices. However, critics have argued that JSAs represent little more than a form of concession bargaining and merely help employers to secure restructuring during recession.

2.4   TRAINING AND LABOUR MARKET POLICY

Vocational and labour market training is a policy area that almost by definition involves employers and employees. It is, therefore, to be expected that policies and practices at the national, industrial, company and workplace level are subject to 'dialogue' between representative organisations. Equally, it is not surprising if policies and practices are subject to negotiation and/or joint formation, and that those policies and practices that are agreed are subject to some form of joint regulation and/or administration. The degree of formality and therefore the kind of institutional structures might vary, but both employers and employees have a close interest in outcomes. This section is concerned with vocational training as provided by employers, both for young people starting their working lives and for adults, and as provided by the state, in the form of publicly supported training for people without jobs and for those seeking a job change. With respect to the training provided by employers, its contribution to the promotion of economic competitiveness is to be noted. With respect to the training provided by the state, the role of the social partners in the administration and formulation of labour market policy is of especial interest.

Table 2.5 captures the main features of national provision. Substantial differences with respect to training policy between the nine countries in this study are not as great as they are with respect to many other areas of policy formulation. This is because training, unlike many other areas in which employers and employees have an interest, is one in which negotiation is more likely to imply 'win–win' rather than 'zero-sum' outcomes – that is, sound training policies and practices produce benefits for all. Nevertheless, the divide between Austria and the UK appears large.

Social Partnership and Workplace Training

Austria has, as to be expected, a highly developed system of vocational training that reflects its social partnership tradition. Initial vocational education in the form of apprenticeships, which is governed by complex laws and regulations, is subject to social partnership through consultations held by the controlling economics ministry. In the industrial as opposed to the political domain, issues such as apprentice pay (or rather 'allowance') rates are the subject of collective bargaining. While it is generally agreed that the 'dual' apprentice training system has been a substantial contributor to the low levels of youth unemployment Austria has experienced, it should also be recognised that, over the last decade, vocational schools have become as important a source of initial training as apprenticeships.

Apprenticeship schemes, controlled or jointly regulated by unions, used to be of considerable importance in the **United Kingdom**. However, already in the 1970s this apprenticeship system was in decline, and in the 1980s, with unions increasingly on the defensive, joint regulation of vocational training depended on whether or not an individual company saw it as valuable. The parity training boards, which had been established in the 1960s to oversee sectoral training needs, had all been abolished by 1990. Where industry training arrangements were continued, they were dominated by employers, as

Table 2.5 Social partnership/dialogue and training

	Company and workplace activities	Public policy bodies	Recent changes
Austria	Works councils (where present) oversee apprentice training and adult training	Apprenticeship training through involvement in social partnership structures of relevant ministries; adult training mainly provided in organisations run respectively by employers (higher management and self-employed)and employee interest groups	Since 1994 labour market service set up as agency with joint (tripartite) administration of active labour market policy
Germany	Works councils (where present) oversee apprentice training and adult training	Joint (tripartite) administration of active labour market policy Joint administration of vocational training institute Adult training provided in organisations run respectively by employers (higher management) and employee interest groups	
Netherlands	Increasingly subject of collective bargaining at sectoral and company level	Joint (tripartite) administration of active labour market policy since 1990	1995 powers of joint boards reduced to setting key policies; also no side now has a veto and decisions can be taken on a simple majority
Sweden	Increasingly subject of collective bargaining at sectoral and company level	Joint (bipartite) administration of active labour market policy with dominant role for trade unions	1992 administration made tripartite with equal number of reps from parliament and people having relationship with, but not appointed by, industry and labour

France	Since 1982 obligation to negotiate at sectoral level on training	Since early 1970s almost all laws on training based upon prior intersectoral agreements	1994 intersectoral agreement setting up parity organisations governing use of industry training funds; 1995 intersectoral agreement on employment and training contracts for youth
Italy	Emergence of joint committees on training at company level	Consultative structures only with respect to labour market policy	1996 pact for employment and earlier pacts included agreements on employment and training contracts for youth
Spain	Accords promote negotiations at sectoral and regional levels	Consultative structures only with respect to labour market policy. Adult training provided in organisations run respectively by employers (higher management) and employee interest groups	National Accord on Continuous Training for 1993–96 renewed as National Accord on Vocational Training for 1997–2000
Ireland	Increasingly subject of collective bargaining at sectoral and company level	Joint (tripartite) administration of national training authority and statutory industry committees. Adult training provided in organisations run respectively by employers (higher management) and employee interest groups	Participation in discussion of education and training policy through Social Partnership process
UK		Abolition of joint (tripartite) managed state labour market policy/training authority 1985; subsequent replacement by employer-led local training councils	Union-national training authority accord on training leading to national 'bargaining for skills' project

were the newly established, area-based agencies charged with the execution of government training policy.

Much of the world looks to the German system of vocational training as one of the cornerstones of Germany's success in competing in the world by producing high quality, high value-added products (Streeck, 1992a; Bertelsmann Stiftung/Hans-Böckler-Stiftung, 1998). As in Austria, vocational training in **Germany** is subject to social partnership control, in this case in the form of a national institute for training under parity control. Here, training standards are established and monitored, and here, too, is the place for discussion about adaptation of the system and developing new areas of training to meet the changing requirements of the economy and technology. Employers' associations and trade unions from the relevant sectors contribute technical expertise, as well as representing the more 'political' interests of their constituencies. Apprentice allowances are subject to collective bargaining, but at the workplace level, training is primarily the responsibility of the employer. With respect to further training that is directed to meeting the organisation's needs, the employer takes the initiative. Works councils have co-determination rights with respect to training, but their role is largely reactive. The limited involvement of representatives of workers' interests in training issues does not reflect these bodies' lack of concern, but rather the way in which there is in general a high level of agreement about policy and objectives, and this enables unions and works councils to concentrate upon other matters. In general, it can be said that, at the workplace level, employee representatives are primarily concerned with being informed about, rather than trying to shape, what is happening. Skill acquisition is seen as positive, as being an investment in the future and in growth or, at worst, as a means of enhancing job security. Usually the involvement of works councils in an organisation's training policy becomes pronounced only when new skills have implications for the organisation of work and, ultimately, for how many people continue to be employed (Gruenewald et al., 1998).

The importance of skill acquisition and development has made training a subject of greater concern for employers and employee representatives in countries where, traditionally, industrial relations had other concerns. In **Spain**, a national agreement on training signed by the social partners and government in 1993 established a framework for continuous training for those in work. Concrete developments have been more limited, however. Since 1982, training has been legally enshrined as a subject for collective bargaining in **France**, and agreements have been reached in a large number of sectors. Use of the training funds collected by statutory levy has, since 1994, been subject to administration by sector-level parity bodies. Nevertheless, employers, in whose hands the initiation of most workplace and company-level training lies, generate applications for funds. Under co-determination legislation in **Sweden**, and as a consequence of the growth of workplace-level trade union activity in that country over the past 20 years or so, education and skill formation and, related to this, new forms of work organisation, have become a central issue in consultation and negotiation between employers and employee representatives, both at workplace and higher levels. A recent agreement covering the metalworking industry, which has a 'leadership' role, has set up a bipartite committee to initiate, support and monitor continuous training projects at company level.

Until the 1980s, trade unions in the **Netherlands** had not been active in the workplace. Employers, in return for recognising sectoral and intersectoral negotiations, had maintained their prerogative, and although the law provided for statutory works councils, the competence of the latter was limited. By the end of the 1980s, however, workplace activity had become increasingly important. A consequence of the concern of intersectoral accords and sectoral collective agreements with employment promotion and the enhancement of competitiveness was not only the introduction of flexibility but also training on to the bargaining agenda. Appropriate actions and steps to be taken with respect to both flexibility and training could be determined only at the sectoral and workplace level. The involvement of employees and their representatives in company and workplace level training has also received recognition in **Ireland** through the social partnership process. Here, the national understandings have recognised not only that workers are the joint owners of skills but also that increasing the skills base is an important contributor to the achievement of the broader objective of improving competitiveness. This too has led to a series of initiatives to increase the quantity, quality and effectiveness of training at company as well as national level.

Social Partnership and Labour Market Training

A presumed typical feature of neo-corporatist European countries has been a semi-autonomous agency under some form of tripartite control responsible for the execution of active labour market policy. Germany was often presented as a classic example of such an approach, so too was Sweden. **Austria**, perhaps somewhat surprisingly, adopted a tripartite administration of labour market services only in 1994. On the other hand employment policy had always been subject to discussion under social partnership, as had the active labour market policy initiatives of the labour ministry. Table 2.5 also shows that the Netherlands, like Austria, was relatively late in establishing labour market services as a separate agency with a tripartite administrative board, and that **Ireland** now appears to be following a continental European model.

As might be expected, since the early 1980s, joint regulation of labour market services was being eliminated in the **United Kingdom**. In 1985, the government abolished the tripartite Manpower Services Commission and replaced it by the government-controlled Training Agency. In 1990, this, too, was abolished and replaced by area-based Training and Enterprise Councils (TECs) that are dominated by the interests of private business. Two-thirds of their board membership has to consist of senior managers from the private sector (although representatives of the public sector, education, local authorities, voluntary organisations and unions can fill the remaining seats). Such structures were assumed to make labour market programmes more relevant to the needs of the economy (Mosley and Degen, 1994).

Although joint governance of labour market boards is associated with neo-corporatism, some of the neo-corporatist countries have also drawn back from such an approach. In the early 1990s, the dominant role of the social partners on the Labour Market Board (AMS) was drastically reduced in **Sweden**. This followed the withdrawal of business groups from their participation in centralised wage-determining processes (see section above on decentralisation of bargaining). The numerical dominance of the unions on the governing board disappeared, and both employers' associations and unions lost the right of nominating members to that board. Their interests have henceforth been represented indirectly, through the nomination of members having a relationship to industry or labour. Equally, having initially established a labour market authority external to the ministry, on the grounds that it would be more responsive to the needs of the labour market, the government of the **Netherlands** retreated. After only four years, the government decided that the body it had set up was 'too close' to employers and unions. In making policy and managing the activities of the authority, the governing boards were seen to be too 'insider' oriented and as paying insufficient attention to promoting the employment of the disadvantaged and excluded – the task that was 'in the public interest'. Accordingly, in 1995, the responsibility of the governing board was reduced to one of setting key policies with respect to which decisions could henceforth be made on a majority basis rather than through consensus. Furthermore, professional managers were given much more freedom in the execution of policies (Visser and Hemerijck, 1997).

With respect to the formulation, rather than the administration, of training programmes that were elements of active labour market policy, the role of intersectoral agreements is of importance in two countries in particular. Active labour market policy is considered a subject fit for discussion and negotiation under the terms of social partnership in **Ireland**, while the 1993 accord in **Spain** set up the framework for the government to take initiatives on training for people without work. More concrete steps are those which have been enshrined in special agreements in France and, to a lesser extent, Italy. In **France**, since the early 1970s, it has been the practice for legislation on vocational training to reflect the terms of previously made intersectoral agreements. Already in the 1980s, there were a series of initiatives designed to respond to unemployment, and particularly youth unemployment, which led to arrangements promoting employment coupled with training for those having difficulty entering work. The most recent of such agreements is that dating from 1995. In **Italy**, employment and training contracts to assist the integration of young people were one of the elements contained in the 1996 Pact for Employment.

Prospects

Given the widespread recognition that improving training opportunities and raising the skills of the actual and potential workforce benefits an economy as a whole, it is unsurprising that in many European countries steps are being taken to set up, expand and appropriately direct training activities. It is equally unsurprising that, in doing so, they call upon the interests of those most directly involved – business and employees and their representatives. Training appears to offer a largely undisputed scope for social partnership. Table 2.6 shows this.

Table 2.6   Current issues for social partnership and training

Austria	Further development of workplace practices
	Establishment of tripartite governance for active labour market policy
Germany	Further development of workplace practices
Netherlands	Introduction of union interests in workplace training
	Restraining vested interests with respect to labour market policy
Sweden	Concentration on company level
	Reduction of direct social partnership influence and inefficiency of public training programmes (symbolic policy)
France	Symbolic policy for young people
Italy	Symbolic policy for young people
Spain	Setting up framework
Ireland	Setting up framework and introduction of union interests in workplace training
UK	Gradual but limited reintroduction of union interests into workplace training and governance structures for labour market policy

At different ends of the spectrum of what this means stand, as exemplars, **Germany** and **Spain**. The former has a much-praised system, but all actors in the country recognise the need to maintain and build upon that system. The latter has a distinctly underdeveloped system, but governments, employers and unions recognise the need to develop appropriate structures and practices, and they have announced an intent to work together to do so. Also to be recognised are recent developments in the **United Kingdom**. After years of marginalisation, union representatives began to appear on the boards of Training and Enterprise Councils and to become involved in their work. In 1996, the Trades Union Congress and the central body representing all these councils signed an agreement that stressed the importance of developing the skills of the entire workforce and, with the assistance of public funds, launched a series of local-level projects under the name of 'bargaining for skills'.

Although certain training parameters can be determined nationally, and national standards and certification play an important role in facilitating employee mobility, particular needs and applications have to be determined at a more local level. Accordingly, there has been a tendency for the role of the workplace, and of local actors, to grow. This might involve the participation of employee representatives in determining training needs, but it certainly involves their active support for those initiatives that are being taken.

The importance of social partnership and/or dialogue at local level appears recognised in all the countries studied. At the national level, too, there is recognition of the need to involve peak organisations in policy making and administration. The extent of such organisations' influence, or the exact role they should play, is, as Table 2.6 also shows, a matter where there is less unanimity. Contributions with respect to technical issues are valued, but the contribution that the social partners should make to broader policy formulation is sometimes contested.

In both the **Netherlands** and **Sweden**, the role of business and employee interest groups has been diminished. The justification for this in the Netherlands appears to have been that these actors were capturing the resources of the labour market authorities to satisfy their immediate constituencies rather than a wider social need. In Sweden, by contrast, the employers withdrew as part of a strategic review of their involvement in labour market policy. The efficiency of Swedish active labour market policy, including retraining programmes, had in any case been increasingly called into question (for a review, see Forslund and Krüger, 1997). The relationship between an awareness of this lack of effectiveness and the restructuring of policy governance organisations is unclear, but restructuring seems to occur at a time of more widespread disenchantment with 'traditional' ways of doing things.

The contribution to combating youth unemployment made by the sort of special training programmes that grew out of intersectoral agreements and pacts, such as those implemented in **France** and **Italy**, is also somewhat uncertain. There is little doubt that such interventions have an important symbolic role, in that they are indicators that governments, employers and unions are concerned about a problem. If they do not bring tangible results, they might, however, diminish the legitimacy of their initiators.

2.5 SOCIAL SECURITY

Social security, like training and labour market policy, is an area in which the social partners are involved in a policymaking, executive or overview capacity. There is a simple justification for this. In most countries, public social insurance benefits are financed by employer and employee contributions. Employers and employees, through their representatives, therefore feel confident in requesting some element of control over how their money is managed. In addition, it is not unusual to find states that wish to devolve responsibility for certain specialist tasks to those who have a closeness to the subject and, therefore, a perceived expertise and/or sensitivity. Self-administration of social security is consistent with the socialist principle of a 'withering away of the state' and, as such, was presented as a hallmark of its achievement in many of the countries of pre-transition Eastern Europe and in the Soviet Union. It is also a distinguishing feature of the supposedly 'neo-corporatist' states of western Europe.

Intensive involvement of associations representing business and employees in social security policy making is exemplified in the case of **Austria**. This involvement covers the sickness insurance, the workers' compensation and the pensions insurance schemes. The 1994 establishment of a labour market services agency added the un-employment insurance scheme to this list. Of all these benefits, pensions are by far the most important because the Austrian welfare state is very much a pensioners' welfare state (Esping-Andersen, 1997). This is partly because low levels of unemployment have placed relatively few demands on the unemployment benefits system and partly because of simple demographics, combined with a relatively generous old age pension system. In addition, early retirement pensions have long been used in Austria as a means of holding down 'open' unemployment.

Amongst the countries included in this study, the **United Kingdom** is the most unlike Austria. The United Kingdom, together with Ireland, is the only country with a strongly redistributive social security system whereby, once eligibility criteria have been met, there is no link between the level of contributions and the level of wages. The main social security systems in both these countries are the administrative responsibility of the state alone. In the UK, furthermore, no effort is made to involve business or employee interests in the policy formation process beyond a consultation process that surrounds major reforms and the recognition of the rights of any body to make representations to the executive and the legislature. What is yet more interesting about the UK is that employer-based social security – especially in the form of occupational pensions and occupational sick pay, which are important as sources of income for those retiring and those becoming ill – are relatively undeveloped with respect to social partnership. They tend to be seen as benefits given by the employer rather than benefits that are the subject of collective bargaining. Here, the UK is different from **Ireland**, where trade unions have been more forthright in seeking to extend the subject matter of collective bargaining to include pensions and sickness benefits. In the UK, legislation requires company pension schemes to include members on their trustee boards, but unions themselves have no voice in scheme governance unless the sponsoring company invites it.

Social Partnership in Administration

The role of the social partners in the social security policy formulation process in the nine countries is summarised in Table 2.7, below. Given its frequent designation as a 'neo-corporatist' society, **Sweden** is unusual in the limited role given to the social partners in the social security system. The trade unions administer the unemployment insurance system, which is one of the explanations for the very high level of trade union membership in that country, but have little say over the eligibility, benefits or contributions that apply to that system. Such decisions are taken by parliament and in the 1990s governments of both the right and left of centre made cuts in the benefit rate (Vartiainen, 1998). Neither unions nor employers' associations have a role in the administration of other benefits, and their participation in policy making is limited. This last is considered the prerogative of parliament. Thus, in the mid-1990s the Swedish government initiated a major reform of the pension system which dramatically changed pension entitlements and the way in which the pension was to be calculated, and introduced an element of individual funding as well (for details, see Ministry of Health and Social Affairs, 1998). In making reform, the government acknowledged the need for consensus, but sought to achieve it by enlisting the consent of all the major parties in parliament rather than by

Table 2.7 Social security structures and social partnership

	Administrative responsibilities	Recent changes in role	Trade-offs
Austria	Joint administration of social security schemes for employees	Continuous involvement in social security reform via social partnership process	
Germany	Joint administration of state social security schemes for employees	Excluded from involvement in recent pension reform	
Netherlands	Joint administration of state social security schemes for employees	Largely removed from this role 1994	
Sweden	Unions administer unemployment insurance	Excluded from involvement in 1997 major pension reform	
France	Joint administration of state social security schemes for employees	Collective agreement on unemployment benefit reform 1992	
Italy	Not applicable	1995 major pension reform based on agreement between unions and government	1998 speed up of reform based on further agreement and in return for legislation for 35-hour week
Spain	Not applicable	Ad hoc agreements between government and unions on specific elements of social security 1995 agreement set up permanent bipartite commission to be consulted on draft laws	
Ireland	No involvement in state social security system, limited involvement in company schemes	Participation in discussion of future social security policy through Social Partnership process	Extension of pensions through collective bargaining
UK	No involvement in state social security system, almost no involvement in company schemes		

entering into negotiations with the social partners. The latter were merely, and as the government saw fit, informed or consulted.

More in the classic neo-corporatist mould, in that they give an executive role to the social partners in the management of social security, are **Germany** and **France**. In each of these countries, there exist joint administrative boards overseeing the principal social security systems. In Germany, as in Sweden, it is parliament that is responsible for making social security law, although in France the parity organisation governing the unemployment compensation system has a rule-making competence. Since 1958, it had been the task of the social partners to negotiate adaptations of the benefit system to the needs of the labour market, or – especially over the past 15 years or so – to the needs of the government to constrain public expenditure. Products of this process have been agreements, dating from the early 1970s, that have facilitated early retirement and, more recently, a 1992 agreement that reduced benefits, especially for the long-term unemployed. The **Netherlands** also based its social security schemes around autonomous bipartite boards although the fact that these also had rule-making powers led to major reforms (see below).

In **Germany** major decisions, such as pension reform, but not short-term adjustments of, say, the unemployment compensation scheme, were considered to require not merely consensus amongst the political parties but also amongst all other major social groups including unions and employer organisations. The process surrounding the so-called '1992 Pension Reform', which was enacted in 1989 (Schmaehl, 1993), was not dissimilar to the process surrounding the 1997 pension reform in **Austria,** in that it involved extensive consultation and a quest for unanimity amongst all major social and political actors. The difference with Austria was that such a consultation process was less continuous and institutionalised in Germany, and proved to be dispensable.

Excluding the Social Partners

Since the very beginnings of a public social security system in the **Netherlands**, self-administration had been at its heart. One of the most prominent manifestations of self-administration was the tripartite Social Security Council (with government nominees in a smaller proportion) which had an overview over the unemployment, sickness and disability insurance systems. Below this was a series of bipartite Industry

Insurance Associations that managed different elements of social security on a sector-by-sector basis. Although responsibility for laying down the framework of the social security schemes, and the setting of contributions and benefits, lay with the government, the Social Security Council had discretion to interpret rules. Of importance here was the rule governing eligibility for disability benefits. Formally and informally, the Council agreed that full disability benefits could be granted to those with even a minor disability if no suitable job was available for them in the local labour market. The award of disability pensions became the favoured way for dealing with workforce restructuring and reduction, since the benefits were higher than those granted to workers made unemployed and were not time limited. By the mid-1980s, the employment rate of men over 50 in the Netherlands was amongst the lowest in Europe, and the cost of early retirement pensions was enormous.

The government intervened in the late 1980s to cut benefit rates and to put an end to the right to full disability benefits 'for labour market reasons', but it failed to stem entry into early retirement. There was widespread concern with the possibility of the Netherlands 'being sick' and, in practical terms, with what appeared to be an ever-increasing ratio of beneficiaries to contributors. A parliamentary commission of inquiry concluded that policy and practice defended vested interests (both those of employers and employees) rather than managing social security in the interests of society and the economy. The result was legislation in 1994 which abolished existing structures, substantially reducing the power of the social partners to be involved in anything more than a distant advisory role and delegating programme delivery, administration and case management to independent executive bodies (Visser and Hemerijck, 1997).

In **Germany**, what occurred was not the fundamental restructuring of institutions to reduce the role of the social partners, but rather the abandonment of what had come to be seen as the established process for determining major policy change. Demographic change threatened further substantial rises in contribution rates for the retirement pension scheme, but in the short term, too, a government committed to maintaining competitiveness was unwilling to contemplate even the small rise in pension contribution rates that seemed likely for 1997. To avoid such an increase, in 1997, the government, with the general agreement of all actors, increased VAT by one percentage point and directed the resources raised into the pension system. However, and in the wake of the partial failure of the original Alliance for Jobs in 1996, the government also took steps to reduce the increases in contributions that were predicted for coming decades. It accelerated the phasing out of early retirement that had been enacted in 1989, legislated for reform and cut back the scope of contribution credits. A new Pension Reform Law of 1997 went further. It cut the pension replacement rate, cut eligibility for disability pensions and their value, and further reduced the access to early pensions for unemployment and for women (Palik, 1997).

The 1997 law. was enacted despite the objections of the opposition political parties and the trade unions. In proceeding as it did, the government is widely considered to have broken the social consensus which had surrounded the formulation of the 1989 and all previous pensions legislation. The cutbacks in opportunities for early retirement were strongly criticised in the light of the poor labour market situation. However, as in the Netherlands, the way in which employers and unions jointly used the pension system to deal with unemployment, and the way in which costs of redundancy and restructuring were transferred to the public purse, have also been widely acknowledged (Rösner, 1996).

Pacts and Trade-offs

Contrary experiences were to be found elsewhere. In the same way that social pacts and intersectoral accords had been used to tackle issues of wage and employment policy, so too, in some countries, did they play a part in some of the reforms of social security policy. Since the mid-1980s, the government in **Spain** has concluded a series of agreements with the trade unions on specific elements of social security, especially concerning the coverage of unemployment benefit and uprating unemployment and pension benefits, each with only a limited degree of permanence. More profound, however, have been developments in Italy and Ireland.

The 1995 pension legislation in **Italy** was the product of a long series of negotiations with the major union confederations. This process started in 1992, and although it was temporarily interrupted by the brief accession of a right of centre government in 1994, it resulted in reform that was at least as radical as that of Sweden. It, too, involved the move from a 'defined benefit' system to a 'notional defined contribution system', but it supplemented this with drastic cuts of early retirement opportunities (Mundo, 1998). Under pressure to meet the Maastricht convergence criteria, the government sought to bring forward the date at which the reforms would be effective and to restrict the level of and entitlement to pension benefits yet further. This entailed further negotiation, since the unions, with the support of their parliamentary allies on whom the government relied, sought to extract a price – namely, that the government would legislate to impose a 35-hour working week. In this they were successful, although at the cost of alienating the business interest groups, which not only objected to their minimal involvement in the pension reform process but also were fundamentally opposed to across-the-board working time reductions.

Social security reform has been broached in the 'Social Partnership' accords in **Ireland,** again as part of the broader agreement on the way forward for economic and social policy. The latest accord refers to a National Pensions Policy Initiative, which, following wide-ranging consultation, will produce recommendations on the future development of a national pensions policy. However, since the country's demographic structure is rather different from that of most of the other European Union countries, concern with pension reform has been much less to the fore in Ireland. Instead, measures to alleviate social exclusion have been prominent. In 1997, and arising from the ongoing consultation process, the government set up a National Anti-Poverty Strategy to address five key themes: unemployment, particularly long-term unemployment; educational disadvantage; income adequacy; regenerating disadvantaged urban communities with concentrations of poverty; and tackling poverty in rural areas.

Prospects

The different experiences of European countries are worth remarking upon. On first sight, **Austria** appears to have carried out major reform, involving cutting the replacement rate through restraining pension increases and reducing early retirement opportunities and to have done so with the full support of the social partners. In **Germany**, it was deemed impossible to comply with the partnership process if substantial reform was to be achieved, and in the **Netherlands**, too, success in restraining social security expenditure appeared to require the expulsion of the social partners from their role in policy making and policy administration.

At least one of the countries in the study, the **United Kingdom**, enacted a major pension reform – in 1986 – without any attempt to engage in dialogue or negotiation (which is not to say that the reform was either necessary or did not generate problems). In **Sweden**, although consensus amongst the political parties was sought, reform was not made conditional on the agreement of the social partners.

Although the political implications for the 'German model' of the 1997 pension reform, or for the 'Dutch model' of the 1994 social security reform, cannot be overlooked, such breaks with social partnership might sometimes be necessary. The social partnership based reform of **Austria** has been criticised as 'too weak and taking effect too late' by the expert who had been commissioned to advise the government on how it might proceed (Prof. Dr. Bert Rürup, quoted in *Kurier*, 5 October 1997).[2] Neo-corporatist, social partnership-like decision-making processes are recognised as being good at achieving incremental change, when the direction of change is clear (see Streeck, 1992b, with respect to corporate governance). They are less able to cope with the need to make 'paradigmatic change' or major changes in direction. Table 2.8 notes this.

Table 2.8   Challenges to social security

Austria	Early 1990s, future	Budget cuts hitting social benefits, adequacy of long-term pension reform
Germany	1997, future	Lack of consensus on pension reform process
Netherlands	Reform without involvement of social partners	
Sweden	Reform without involvement of social partners	
France	Current/ongoing	Union refusal to consider substantial reform, especially funding or privatisation
Italy	Current/ongoing	Tying pension reform to shorter working time and excluding employers
Spain	Current/ongoing	Confidence rebuilding in 1996 pacts after failures of dialogue in mid 1980s
Ireland	Current/ongoing	Successful realisation of programme to counter social exclusion
UK	Reform without involvement of social partners	

France as much as Austria appears locked into a particular approach to pensions. There, discussion of other than incremental change is effectively taboo. Although in the mid-1990s the government took tentative steps to establish possibilities for a third 'tier' of individual, funded pensions, a change of government – which was in part the consequence of widespread opposition to planned social security retrenchment – has meant that the necessary secondary legislation has never been tabled. The trade unions insist on no deviation from a system based upon 'répartition' (pay as you go) and no contemplation of 'capitalisation' (funding). Thus, throughout the 1980s and 1990s, governments, despite facing a long-term problem of population ageing, have relied on a series of relatively small changes affecting eligibility and replacement rates. At their most radical, they have resorted to increasing the fiscal subsidy to the retirement systems by levying a general solidarity contribution on all incomes (Giorgi, 1998).

The government of **Italy** (and more tentatively the government of **Spain**) has moved in the opposite direction to that of certain other European states, clearly seeing the enrolment of trade union support as vital for successful and speedy reform. However, the Italian government had offered in return a general working time reduction. The successful realisation of the latter will require negotiation between employers and unions (see section above on pay determination and employee relations). Yet in the course of drawing up its pension reform programme, the government had very limited dealings with the employers, who even in the preparation of the 1995 legislation were feeling themselves marginalised. Their alienation was confirmed by the 1997 political settlement that imposed the 35-hour week on them. The government proposes further cuts in the retirement pension – for example, by increasing the retirement age – and the issue is likely to be dealt with by negotiations at central level.

The right to participate in social security policy formulation has, as the unions in Austria have also recognised, its price. Although they were satisfied with the outcome of the pension reform, they had been less content with the savings programmes upon which the government insisted earlier in the 1990s. These programmes, designed to contain public expenditure to help meet the Maastricht convergence criteria, made substantial cuts in other areas of social security, especially family allowances, and unemployment benefits (Tálos and Wörister, 1994; Falkner, 1996). Given their commitment to entry into the European

Union, Austrian trade unions were obliged not only to accept such cuts but also to put their name to them.

Lastly, although this chapter has dealt at length with pensions, it should be remembered that these are not the only item on the social policy agenda. At European Union level, and especially in the post-Essen period, a major concern has been social exclusion. In the individual member countries, this seems scarcely to have been the subject of dialogue or partnership. The notable exception is **Ireland**. Even here, concrete outcomes are to date limited if only because of the recent nature of the concern. Nevertheless, developments in this country merit further attention.

2.6 SUMMARY

The preceding sections provide details of trends in policy formulation processes across a range of areas for each of the nine countries studied: macroeconomic policy, pay determination and employee relations, training and social security. This section summarises experiences and focuses attention on the salient features of the national settings.

In the period under consideration, certain structural changes have affected labour markets across all the member states of the EU. These include the decline of manufacturing and the rise of services, high levels of unemployment, generally declining trade union densities (with some exceptions), increasing participation rates of women, increasing levels of part-time work and so on. In more recent years, efforts to meet the Maastricht criteria and preparations for European Monetary Union have also served to set macroeconomic objectives across all the EU member states. What this chapter has sought to examine are the institutional responses to these common pressures. Table 2.9 presents a clear picture of these relevant developments.

Austria is marked by a sophisticated and long-standing degree of social partnership that has maintained itself remarkably unchanged over recent years, despite mounting pressures. The framework for pay determination is set centrally, with subsequent sector-level bargaining led by metalworking. The negotiation of more flexible working time has been delegated only to sector level, with the unions successfully resisting further decentralisation to the workplace. Training is subject to

Table 2.9 Summary of trends and developments

	Macroeconomic management	Pay determination	Employee relations/ employment contracts	Training	Social security
Austria	No change; continuous discussions between government and social partners	No change; centralised framework, sector-level bargaining	Centralisation; limited delegation to sectors (e.g. working time)	Recent formal tripartism. Integral part of management of competitiveness with respect to labour market services	Long-standing tripartite administration. Social partners accept cuts
Germany	Tradition of unilateral government action, but Alliance for Jobs established 1998	Sector-level bargaining; increasing decentralisation to workplace (management of flexibility)	Sector-level bargaining; increasing decentralisation to workplace (management of flexibility)	Long-standing tripartism. Integral part of management of competitiveness	Development from consensual to unilateral decision making. Long-standing tripartite administration
Netherlands	Unilateral government action. Information and consultation over objectives	Sector-level bargaining; increasing decentralisation to workplace (management of flexibility)	Sector-level bargaining; increasing decentralisation to workplace (management of flexibility)	New component of supply-side corporatism. Social partnership kept out of administration	Cuts introduced only through downgrading consultation with social partners
France	No change. Unilateral government action	Sector level, but delegation to company level	Sector level, but delegation of certain subjects (e.g. working time) to 'lowest possible level'	Long-term joint regulation; not yet penetrated to workplace level	No change. Long-standing bipartism. Consensus has led to inaction

Italy	Unilateral government action. Information and consultation over objectives	Rationalisation of structures; trade-offs on areas like pay indexation	Rationalisation of structures	Generally cosmetic activity	Major trade-offs at intersectoral level (e.g. pension reform for 35-hour week)
Spain	Unilateral government action	Eventual failure of intersectoral pay agreements in 1980s	Intersectoral agreements on non-pay issues (e.g. April Accords)	Recent establishment of framework	Establishment of basic frameworks
Sweden	Unilateral government action	Decentralisation to sector	No change. Acceptance of flexible working (supply-side corporatism)	Long-standing supply-side corporatism	Unilateral decision making
Ireland	Recent development of social partnership	Intersectoral restraints through social partnership; trade-offs on taxation etc.	Encouragement of workplace social partnership	Recognition of importance by social partners	Social partners recognise problem of social exclusion
UK	Unilateral government action. Abolition of NEDC	Decentralisation to company and workplace; development of unilaterally imposed pay systems	1998 White Paper recognises need for social partnership and supply-side corporatism	Union involvement in TECs and bargaining for skills	No activity yet

extensive consultation with employers and labour while social security has been administered on a tripartite basis for many years. The country carried out a major reform of pensions through the process of social partnership in 1997.

In **Germany,** where social partnership has never been as extensive as in Austria, the system has also come under strain, particularly at workplace level. Both pay and other employee relations issues – traditionally negotiated at sector level – have been increasingly delegated to the workplace. This trend has prompted prolonged discussion about whether or not this means the end of the German model. Training remains subject to long-standing tripartite regulation, but by contrast the government enacted pensions reform on a unilateral basis, thereby breaking the social consensus on the issue that had existed until then. Social security administration remains under tripartite administration, however.

Developments in the **Netherlands** have been broadly comparable. The social partners are informed and consulted over the objectives of macroeconomic policy, but the government takes unilateral action. Decentralisation of pay determination has also taken place, but as the result of a central agreement in 1982 to do so (rather than by default, as in Germany). Decentralisation extends to other aspects of employee relations too, such as working time and employment security, as well as training. Administration of active labour market policy, including training, has been based on tripartite boards since 1990. However, the government reduced the role of these joint boards in 1995 on the grounds that they were too 'insider-oriented'. With respect to social security as well, the government has introduced cuts by means of downgrading consultative arrangements with the social partners.

The government controls macroeconomic policy in **France,** though the social partners are duly invited to submit their opinions. Since 1982, government legislation has encouraged company and workplace collective bargaining as the most appropriate means of pay determination, though the sector remains important. Similarly, legislation has ensured that working time flexibility is also negotiated at the 'lowest possible level' and has supported appropriate institutional change to support this. With respect to training, since the early 1970s almost all legislation has been based on prior intersectoral agreement. State social security schemes for employees have been jointly administered for many years, and in 1992 unemployment benefit was reformed by collective agreement. However, the unions have blocked the structural reform of pensions.

A major intersectoral agreement in **Italy** in 1993 introduced an annual round of consultation with the social partners over macroeconomic policy. In the same way, a series of intersectoral social pacts has reformed the structure of collective bargaining and workplace union channels or representation in order to rationalise the levels at which pay and employee relations issues may be bargained. Joint committees on training are emerging at company level though consultation takes place on bodies regulating active labour market policy. Employment, training contracts and other labour market issues have been covered on several occasions since 1992 through the negotiation of intersectoral pacts. Pensions were reformed in 1995 following lengthy negotiations between the government and unions, and, under pressure to bring forward the date on which the reforms were to come into force, the government traded this off with legislation to introduce the 35-hour week.

Spain bears a number of aspects in common with Italy. Government consults the social partners over certain macroeconomic objectives following relevant agreement in 1992. A series of intersectoral pacts in the 1980s set the framework for pay determination, though this system had collapsed by the latter part of the decade. Since then, intersectoral agreements have focused on a range of other issues, such as the reform of collective bargaining, the system of disputes mediation and the cost of dismissals. Collective bargaining takes place principally at sector or regional level, though workplace bargaining is increasingly significant. An intersectoral agreement on continuous training, signed in 1992, was renewed in 1996 and establishes a national framework that promotes negotiations at sectoral and regional level. A series of agreements between government and unions since 1985 has covered specific areas of social security.

Macroeconomic policy is undertaken unilaterally in **Sweden.** The most significant change in relation to social dialogue in recent years is the demise of intersectoral pay negotiations, following withdrawal by the employers from the system in 1992. Pay is now negotiated at sector level, though as in other countries metalworking takes the lead in setting the expected rate. The framework of employee relations remains set by landmark legislation adopted in the 1970s, and at workplace level there has long been acceptance of flexible forms of working. Administration of active labour market policy is now carried out on a tripartite basis, with members of parliament and other people associated with industry and labour, but not appointed by them. Training is increasingly a subject for collective bargaining at sectoral and company level. Social security matters are subject to unilateral decisions taken by government.

Ireland is characterised by a recent development of social partnership. Since 1987, wide-ranging tripartite intersectoral agreements have been agreed at three-yearly intervals. They are statements of common understanding and have no status other than that accorded to them by the signatories. However, they have covered pay, taxation, social welfare, education and health policy. Progress on implementation is monitored by a number of committees, including the National Economic and Social Forum, which also represents interests outside the tripartite framework. The national training authority and statutory training industry committees are run on a tripartite basis, and training itself is increasingly being negotiated at sectoral and company levels. The social partners are not involved in the state social security system, and the unions have only a limited role in company pension schemes.

Lastly, the **United Kingdom** is the country where systems of social dialogue are the least formal. Government decisions on macroeconomic policy are taken alone. The National Economic and Development Council, which once acted as a forum for consultations over such policy, was abolished in 1992. Pay determination has decentralised from sector level down to company and workplace levels, though the new government has, following a process of advice and consultation, introduced a national minimum wage. In its 1998 White Paper, the new government recognised the need for social partnership and supply-side corporatism, though it has retained all the anti-union legislation enacted by its predecessor. The unions have become more involved in the employer-led Training and Enterprise Centres, though there is no social partnership involvement in social security. There is limited involvement of unions on the boards of company pension schemes.

The establishment of general patterns is difficult. Depending on which features are selected for comparison, it is possible to group countries that might otherwise have looked quite dissimilar. For example, Italy and Spain have both rationalised their industrial relations systems through the use of social pacts involving new and complex trade-offs. The Netherlands and Ireland have also used intersectoral understandings to investigate new trade-offs that have been beneficial to their economies. France and Sweden have generally given primacy to government rather than the social partners in the formulation of social and economic policy.

Nevertheless, from the examination of the experiences of the nine countries, the following general conclusions can be drawn.

- There is a general tendency, more or less pronounced, and starting at different levels according to country, towards decentralisation of industrial relations and labour market regulation.
- Countries with neo-corporatist institutions have often come under pressure, and in some countries tripartite bodies and negotiation and consultation structures and procedures have been downgraded or even abolished entirely.
- However, central agreements – or social pacts – have been concluded often under conditions of crisis in a number of countries in recent years and, in some, the success of an initially ad hoc arrangement has led to a degree of institutionalisation.
- Social pacts have often allowed the negotiation of trade-offs between the social partners across complex social and labour policy areas (not just on pay and working time, but also training, pensions and fiscal policy, amongst others).
- Decentralisation is therefore not a zero-sum model of social and labour regulation. The reorganisation of the powers and competences of the social partners at varying levels may allow them the leeway necessary to negotiate and apply the details of policies at company or workplace level that have been agreed as broad frameworks at higher levels.

NOTES

1. The SER was described to one of the authors as the place where 'zero sum games are played' – where each side feels that what it concedes is a loss to itself but a gain to the other side.
2. According to one commentator, 'the role of the social partners in bringing about

the pension reform was eminent and they succeeded, in particular, in moderating the Government's aspirations. In this they were united. According to experts, little remained of the original plan ... In the "competition" between reducing early retirement for the sake of the pension system's finances and using early retirement as a measure to reduce or conceal unemployment, the latter aim clearly remained dominant' (EIRO, AT9711144F).

3 Economic Performance in the Nine Countries

The previous chapter has outlined the nature of the institutions governing social partnership and social protection across the nine EU member states covered in this book. It examined trends and developments in these institutions with respect to macroeconomic policy, pay determination and employee relations, training and social security.

This chapter investigates the relationship between these institutions and their impact on economic performance. It begins by reviewing the existing literature on the subject, and then proceeds to discuss a number of methodological difficulties involved in analysing the relationships concerned. It examines and explains the relevant indicators of performance to be used, as well as the time series for examination. The chapter then presents an analysis of the countries covered before drawing some general conclusions.

3.1 FINDINGS OF OTHER STUDIES

A number of theorists have attempted to relate the nature of social institutions to indicators of economic performance, such as growth rates. Worthy of note is a cross-national study that tested the 'Olson theory' of the cloying effect of exclusive interest groups – that is, interest groups covering a narrow section of the population that focus on their own advantage to the exclusion of wider considerations. Choi (1983) found that in countries where long-established groups of this type existed, growth rates were lower. Along rather different lines, Knack and Keefer (1997) sought to establish whether countries with a higher level of 'social capital' – which includes notions of social justice, trust and tolerance – performed better. They constructed indicators of social capital by focusing on data on interpersonal trust and civic engagement gathered from the World Values Survey (Inglehart et al., 1998), and found that it was positively associated with economic growth (for a review of some of this literature, see Leicht, 1999).

Reference also needs to be made to an ambitious attempt to appraise the merits of social protection and economic flexibility (Blank, 1994). However, this comprised a series of 'partial' analyses in so far as it was made up of separate examinations of, for example, the relationship between employment protection and labour market flexibility, health insurance provision and labour market efficiency, and pension provision and the labour force participation of older people. The limitation of any aggregation of partial analyses is that the relative weight given to particular outcomes is a source of controversy. The obvious example is the trade-off between inflation and unemployment, but equally it can be argued that public pensions, while imposing substantial tax burdens, play an important role in contributing to intergenerational solidarity.

Other attempts to examine the effects of institutions on 'performance' consist largely of two types:

- single country/industry studies of the effects of partnership on firm/workplace productivity; and
- cross-national studies of the impact of 'protection' on economic growth.

The results of these are reported in Tables 3.1a, 3.1b and 3.2 below.

Table 3.1a suggests that 'co-determination' as practised in Germany has a negative impact upon profitability, but that its other effects on innovation and investment can be positive. Results from other countries, where the form of partnership differs greatly from case to case, are shown in Table 3.1b. They show that partnership has, on occasions, been found to have a positive effect on productivity, but they also include indeterminate outcomes. Overall, it has to be concluded that whether or not partnership produces benefits depends on the form it takes and its context.

Table 3.2 gives a very unclear picture, with studies showing benefits from protection being matched by studies showing the reverse.

The results reported in Tables 3.1a, 3.1b and 3.2, as well as being rather inconclusive, have also to be treated with a degree of caution.

Table 3.1a   *Econometric studies of the relationship between partnership and enterprise performance – examples from Germany*

	Svejnar (1982)	Fitzroy and Craft (1985)	Fitzroy and Craft (1990)	Schnabel and Wagner (1992)	Addison et al. (1993)	Schnabel and Wagner (1994)	Addison et al. (1996)	Addison and Wagner (1997)
Subject	Private sector industries	Metalworking industry firms	Metalworking industry firms	Manufacturing firms	Manufacturing firms	Manufacturing firms	Manufacturing firms	Manufacturing firms
Dependent variable	Productivity	Profitability	Product innovation	Product innovation	a. Profitability b. Investment	R & D intensity	a. Profitability b. Product innovation c. Process innovation	a. Profitability b. Product innovation
Determining variable	Works councils	Works councils	Works councils and union density	Works councils	Works councils	Works councils	Works councils	Works councils and works council involvement
Relationship	None or negative	Negative	Negative	Positive	a. Negative b. Positive	Positive	a. Negative b. Positive c. Indeterminate	Indeterminate
Significance	Not significant	Significant	Significant	Not significant	a. Significant b. Not significant	Significant	a. Significant b. Significant	Not significant

Sources: all studies referred to in this table, except for Addison and Wagner (1997), are taken from Addison et al. (1996).

81

Table 3.1b   Econometric studies of the relationship between partnership and enterprise performance – examples from other countries

	Katz et al. (1983)	Katz et al. (1987)	Mitchell et al. (1990)	Cutcher-Greshenfeld (1991)
Subject	USA: Auto industry	USA: Auto industry	USA: private sector businesses	USA: manufacturing plants
Dependent variable	a. Direct labour efficiency b. Product quality	a. Hours input per unit b. Supervisory input	a. Productivity b. Returns	a. Productivity b. Quality
Determining variable	Participative arrangements (QWL)	Participation in decision making with respect to: (i) work organisation (ii) new technology	Non-economic participation	QWL
Relationship	a. Negative b. Positive	a. Positive re (i) and (ii) b. Positive re (i) and (ii)	a. Positive b. Positive	Indeterminate
Significance	a. Not significant b. Significant		a. Significant b. Not significant	Not significant

Note: studies are those of representative (effectively randomly sampled) units without elements of employee ownership.

Cook (1994)	MacDuffie (1995)	Fernie and Metcalf (1995)	Morishima (1991)
USA: manufacturing businesses	USA: automobile plants	UK: medium and large workplaces in trading sector	Japan: large private-sector firms
Net value added per employee	a. Productivity b. Quality	a. Productivity b. Productivity growth	a. Returns b. Productivity c. Labour costs
Work teams with unions and without unions	Team working	(i) Boosting employee involvement (ii) Joint Consultative Committee	Joint Consultation Committees (information sharing)
Positive, but greater effect with unions	a. Positive (if complemented by appropriate production organisation) b. Positive	a. Positive re (i) and (ii) b. Positive re (ii)	a. Positive b. Positive c. Positive
Significant	a. Significant b. Not significant	a. Significant b. Not significant	a. Significant b. Significant c. Significant

Sources: as listed in bibliography.

Table 3.2 Econometric studies of the relationship between social protection and economic performance

	Landau (1985)	Korpi (1985)	Weede (1986)	McCallum and Blaise (1987)	Castles and Dowrick (1990)	Weede (1991)	Nordström (1992)	Hansson and Henrekson (1994)	Personn and Tabellini (1994)	Casey and Gold (1998)
Dependent variable	GDP growth	GDP growth	GDP growth	GDP growth	Total factor productivity growth	Labour productivity growth	GDP growth	Private sector total factor productivity growth	GDP growth	Competitiveness level (IMD index)
Determining variable	Soc sec share	Soc sec share	Initial soc sec share	Initial soc sec share	Initial soc sec share	Initial soc sec share	Initial soc sec share	Soc sec share	Soc sec share	Past soc sec share
Relationship	Positive	Positive	Negative	Positive	Positive	Negative	Negative	Negative	Negative	Positive
Significance	Not significant	Significant	Significant	Significant	Significant	Significant	Significant	Not significant	Significant	Not significant

Note: 'Soc sec share' means 'social security expenditure as a percent of GDP'; a positive relationship suggests that an increase in social security's share of GDP has a beneficial consequence for the dependent variable, and vice versa.

Sources: All studies referred to in this table, except for Casey and Gold (1998), are taken from Atkinson (1995, Table 1); see also below. Casey and Gold, building upon Thompson, 1998, regressed the share of social transfers in GDP for the period 1980–89 (TRANSHR), the percentage change in this in the period 1990–95 (◆TRAN) and the employer social insurance contribution rate for the early 1990s (EMPCONT) on the index of competitiveness (COMP) constructed by the International Institute for Management Development (IMD) for the year 1997 and 1998. The preferred models were:

COMP (EURO) =	EMPCONT	+ TRANSHR	+ ◆TRAN	adjusted r^2
coefficient	-0.864	1.139	0.211	0.457
standard error	(0.273)	(0.623)	(0.226)	
COMP (OECD) =	EMPCONT	+ TRANSHR	+ ◆TRAN	adjusted r^2
coefficient	-0.886	0.855	0.190	0.248
standard error	(0.320)	(0.799)	(0.639)	

where EURO refers to 13 OECD Europe countries (Germany, France, Italy, UK, Austria, Finland, Greece, Iceland, Netherlands, Norway, Spain, Sweden and Switzerland) and OECD to these plus United States, Canada, Japan and Australia.

This is because such exercises often fail to address the problem of 'simultaneity' or 'endogeneity' – that is, the possibility that certain variables are determined by forces operating within the model itself. Thus, with respect to the findings on partnership, two interpretations of an apparent positive association between it and performance can be made:

- either partnership does enhance performance; or
- units that perform 'well' can 'afford' more democratic/humane systems of employment relations.

Equally, a negative association could be explained as:

- units with poor performance searching around for a system of employment relations which might improve their position.

With respect to the findings on 'protection', a positive association could reflect:

- the way in which social protection facilitates the achievement of a higher level of performance; or
- the fact that good performance might make social protection affordable.

Equally, a negative association could be consequent upon:

- protection systems being set up in a period of relative under-development and contributing to rapid growth, but reaching maturity and hence high levels of expenditure at a time when the growth rates slow down as they tend to do in more developed countries (the 'catch-up' effect).

An OECD (1997c) study looked at the impact of collective bargaining structures on performance measured on a number of dimensions. Its findings tended to be favourable to 'neo-corporatist' structures, as the first row of Table 3.3 shows. The second row of Table 3.3 is however rather ambiguous. The negative association between decentralisation and employment growth could imply:

Table 3.3   *Relationship between performance and collective bargaining (macro data)*

Collective bargaining	Performance indicators				
	Unemploy-ment rate	Employ-ment growth	Inflation	Real earnings growth	Earnings inequality
Centralised/ Co-ordinated	Lower *		Lower **		Less *
Decentralising		Lower *			

Note: * significant at 10%, ** significant at 5%

Source: derived from OECD, 1997c (Tables 3.6–8)

- support for the argument that neo-corporatist arrangements are superior; or
- that, in some poorly performing neo-corporatist countries, there has been an attempt to restructure institutions.

3.2   MODELLING THE DETERMINANTS OF PERFORMANCE

Subject to specification of an appropriate, and probably necessarily, composite measure of performance, the establishment of its link with the institutions of partnership/dialogue and protection remains problematic. In very general terms, the impact of institutions upon performance could (building upon Rodrik, 1997) be understood in the following fashion:

performance = f (shocks, institutions, plus other country- and time-specific variables)

Potential components of the left-hand side (the dependent variable) of the model will be discussed later. However, before this is done, attention is directed to the right-hand side terms.

'Shocks' to any country might include the oil price crises of 1973 and 1979 (reflected, for example, in major shifts in terms of trade) or adaptation to new regimes (such as entry into the European Union, particularly for Austria and Sweden, or reunification for Germany).

'Institutions' would cover the system of social partnership/dialogue in the country and the system of social protection. There have been numerous attempts to specify the former, both by economists interested in pay determination and by political scientists interested in governance, and even attempts to present the results in index form. Social protection is conventionally measured by the share of GDP allocated by the state to pensions, unemployment, social assistance and sickness payments, although account might also need to be taken of corporate social welfare – largely collectively bargained but in some cases mandated provision – which supplements state provision. Insofar as the state can mandate certain forms of behaviour (like rules on dismissal) and income transfers (like corporate sick-pay schemes), the costs of these might also justifiably be included as elements both of social partnership and of social protection (Kopits and Craig, 1998). Institutions might also include 'income distribution' – hence the problem of endogeneity referred to earlier. Income distribution has been used by Rodrik (1997) as a proxy for 'latent social conflict'.

Amongst 'other country- and time-specific variables' mention should be made of the relative importance of fiscal transfers within the European Union, particularly those consequent upon the operation of the Common Agricultural Policy (CAP) and the structural funds. Certain EU countries have been substantial net beneficiaries and others net contributors. Of the countries included in this study, two stand out as substantial beneficiaries. These are Ireland, which in the 1990s received transfers equivalent to nearly five per cent of its national product, with the CAP accounting for nearly two-thirds of this, and Spain, which has received over one and a quarter per cent of its national product. Substantial contributors are the Netherlands, Germany and Sweden, each of which have transferred some two-thirds of a percent of national product to other EU countries over the 1990s (see Commission, 1998d).

In so far as attempts have been made to operationalise models and test them using macro-data, certain lessons have been learnt. One is that the relationship between performance and collective bargaining/ negotiating systems is likely to be non-linear – highly centralised and highly decentralised systems appear to perform better. This result is not inconsistent with the Olson theory referred to above. Another is that the direction of causality is not always immediately apparent. This is a restatement of the endogeneity problem discussed above. A classic case is the relationship between social expenditure and growth (as reviewed in Atkinson, 1995). Good performance might make social protection affordable, but social protection facilitates the achievement of a higher level of performance. A similar debate can be held about the desirability of social partnership or dialogue. It can be argued as either a precondition for performance or as a fruit of performance.

This, in turn, raises questions about appropriate 'lags'. Many interventions might have a long pay-off period – health promotion and education being good examples. The promotion of endogenous growth can be seen as an attempt to use 'new' and 'obscure' terminology or 'jargon' to defend a 'statist', high public expenditure-based approach by government. Or it might be seen as recognition that there is a role for the state to provide some public goods, goods which yield returns only in the long term and which markets, interested in individual and short term returns, fail to provide. Equally, the success of the Dutch model of social consultation is widely commented upon. Examination suggests that the rewards of the restraint it generated were a long time in coming. The first major accord was signed in 1982; the growth in jobs followed much later. The whole has been described as a 15-year, ongoing process (Visser and Hemerijck, 1997).

Related to the problem of lags is the problem of appropriate observation periods. First, not all EU or OECD countries are at the same point in the economic cycle. Some of this is subject to capture by what have been referred to as country- and time-specific variables. Second, institutions can be functional in certain periods and dysfunctional in others. The German model was praised throughout much of the 1970s and 1980s but is currently subject to criticism and doubt. The Swedish system in particular, but the German system too, has been analysed in terms of containing the ingredients both of initial 'success' and of subsequent 'failure'. Equally, almost all OECD countries changed elements of their social protection systems in the 1980s. Some of these changes might have had a relatively immediate impact on behaviour – for example, changes in unemployment compensation systems – while others might have had an impact only in the longer term – for example, changes in pension systems. The fact that institutions change means not only that any model would have to apply appropriate lags, but also that the value of any proxying variable changes over time. All this presents a challenge to anyone seeking to establish the link between social partnership/dialogue and protection.

3.3   MEASURING PERFORMANCE

Economic theory, perhaps not surprisingly, has had very little to say about performance in the aggregate sense. In some respects this follows from the concern of theory with utility. The principal, indeed guiding, objective of actors is taken to be the maximisation of utility, but utility itself is not measured. All that is recognised is that in general additional units of utility add less than previous units ('diminishing returns') and that increases in the utility of one actor can diminish the utility of another ('externalities'). When society as a whole is considered, there is a tendency to use Gross Domestic Product (GDP) as a proxy for utility. This, of course, measures only certain dimensions of material wellbeing. Refinement can be made, and one way is to take account of some combination of a country's growth rate, inflation rate, unemployment rate and trade balance.

However, it is possible for any one country to produce high scores with reference to such economic measures but to offend against some observers' notions of success on other grounds. Conventional measures of performance tend to steer well clear of attempting to capture psychological well-being. Nevertheless, in the same way that it might be argued that a 'too uneven' distribution of income is prejudicial to the achievement of good performance, it could also be argued that a society with too much evenness in income distribution is 'under-performing'. Along similar lines, it could be argued that a society lacking democratic involvement by its inhabitants in the macro and micro institutions of which they are a part is also under-performing. The problem is that both 'psychological well-being' and 'democratic involvement' are difficult to calibrate and, where proxies are used, there is not always certainty about what the optimum value of these should be. This is not to say that even such measures as 'unemployment' are unambiguous, but at least most observers would argue that less unemployment (perhaps subject to a NAIRU constraint) was a 'good thing'. By contrast, some would see positive incentive effects and others threats to cohesion in a wider income distribution.

Even if a more restricted approach is taken, which ignores aspects of 'psychological' well-being and concentrates only upon quantifiable, 'economic' aspects, problems arise where composite indicators are used. A popular example of a composite indicator is the 'misery index' of inflation and unemployment. Such an index suggests that there is a trade-off between the two components whereby one percentage point less unemployment has the same 'value' as one percentage point less inflation – a trade-off which has no standing in itself, and does not accord with the relationship between the two variables implied by a conventional Phillips curve.[1] Similar objections may be raised against the 'magic triangle', which sums inflation, unemployment and the trade deficit, whereby the smaller the area of the triangle, the more successful the economy. Yet others (for example, Breuss, 1993 cited in Butschek, 1995) construct a composite indicator using the 'magic square', which brings the growth rate into the summation.[2]

For the purposes of this study, and despite the objections raised above, a variant of the magic square is used to measure performance. In other words:

performance = GDP growth rate − inflation rate − unemployment rate +
(BOP surplus/GDP)

The absolute value of the score generated by this indicator might well be negative because, while growth is usually positive, inflation and unemployment contribute negative elements to the summation, as does any balance of payment deficit. Indeed, for most of the countries in this study, over most of the years, the performance score generated is negative. However, a higher positive value, or a lower negative value, indicates a superior performance, and scores can be compared between countries at any one point in time and within a single country across time. Accordingly, the score can be used to 'benchmark' countries' performance.[3]

Adjustments can be made to the score to take out certain components or to adjust the weighting given to them. This enables simple sensitivity tests to be made. Where this is done, scores have been subject to a simple process of standardisation to make them more directly comparable. The adjustments made are:

(a)   the removal of the contribution of the balance of payments (BOP) element, to take account of some countries, especially Ireland where first very large negative, and subsequently very large positive, balances have been run;

(b)   substituting the 'non-employment rate' – the number of those not in work relative to the population of working age – for the unemployment rate, since the latter fails to reflect 'hidden unemployment' and since employment can be regarded as a good indicator of 'inclusion';

(c)   altering the weights given to the unemployment and inflation elements so that the consequences can, in turn, be seen as treating unemployment as a greater evil than inflation and inflation as a greater evil than unemployment; and

(d)   weighting the score by relative GDP per capita, since a country can appear to perform well according to any of the indicators used so far yet still be very poor.

As well as presenting data for the nine European Union countries that have been the specific object of this study, the score has also been calculated for the United States of America. This is a country where political and economic institutions have never been favourable to a neo-corporatist approach and where markets appear to dominate. Thus, it provides a suitable comparator.

In the study, two time periods were considered:

(a)   1979–89 – from the peak before the onset of the second oil price rise-induced recession to the peak before the post-gulf war recession (that is, a period that looks across a full economic cycle); and

(b)   1992–97 – from the Maastricht Treaty onwards and as EU countries strove to satisfy the convergence criteria for entry into European Monetary Union (that is, a period during which all the EU member states faced similar, self-imposed economic constraints).

The fact that there are two periods means that comparisons over time can be made. The fact that relatively long periods were chosen, and the average performance across the whole of any one period was calculated, means that the effects of any 'exceptional' year are smoothed out.

3.4 RESULTS: THE COUNTRIES COMPARED

The absolute performance score for each of the countries is shown in Table 3.4a. The higher a positive score, or the closer a negative score is to zero, the better the country's performance. Table 3.4b compares each country's score with that of the United States. In Table 3.4b, a negative value means that the United States is performing worse than the country in question, a positive score means that the United States is performing better. The results from the basic analysis are given in Panel 1 of the tables. The following points can be made.

- Germany performed better than all the other countries in the 1980s, although the difference between it and Austria was small. The United States scored considerably less well than these two countries and than Sweden or the Netherlands.
- Between the 1980s and the 1990s, there was an improvement in performance across the majority of countries in the study but a substantial worsening in Germany and no significant improvement in Austria and Spain.
- The greatest improvement in performance between the two periods was shown by Ireland, which also scores the 'best' performance. Other major 'improvers' were the Netherlands, Italy and the USA.
- In the 1990s, Germany and Austria were overtaken by the Netherlands and Ireland. The United States outperformed Germany and only marginally under-performed Austria.
- Spain performed consistently less well than all other countries under investigation.

The first test for sensitivity that was applied was to remove 'trade performance' from the composite performance indicator. The results of such an exercise are shown in Panel 2a. The overall picture is remarkably unchanged. Only two changes are worth noting.

- Excluding 'trade' lowers the absolute scores for Sweden, the Netherlands and Ireland in the second period. In the 1990s, each of these countries ran substantial balance of payments surpluses.
- The running of a positive balance on the external account

Table 3.4a   Absolute performance in selected countries

	Austria	Sweden	Netherlands	Germany	UK	France	Italy	Spain	Ireland	USA
Panel 1: performance (= growth – unemployment – inflation + trade balance)										
mean 79–89	-5.0	-8.1	-6.8	-4.0	-14.4	-14.5	-18.5	-26.3	-24.1	-12.4
mean 92–97	-4.8	-5.4	0.1	-8.9	-10.5	-9.8	-11.1	-24.8	6.0	-6.8
Panel 2a: performance (= growth – unemployment – inflation)										
mean 79–89	-5.2	-9.2	-9.9	-6.7	-14.7	-14.4	-18.1	-26.2	-20.7	-10.5
mean 92–97	-5.0	-10.8	-6.0	-9.7	-9.6	-12.3	-14.7	-24.8	-7.6	-5.5
Panel 2b: performance (= growth – non-employment – inflation + trade balance)										
mean 92–97	-13.3	-2.7	-8.7	-15.9	-11.3	-19.2	-28.6	-35.3	-6.7	-6.8
Panel 3a: performance (as Panel 1) with unemployment worse than inflation										
mean 79–89	-6.6	-8.7	-12.1	-7.6	-19.0	-18.4	-21.4	-34.8	-30.1	-15.8
mean 92–97	-7.0	-11.6	-5.0	-13.7	-15.6	-17.3	-17.8	-37.3	-5.8	-10.3
Panel 3b: performance (as Panel 1) with inflation worse than unemployment										
mean 79–89	-7.2	-13.3	-7.9	-5.6	-17.8	-18.0	-24.7	-30.1	-27.3	-14.5
mean 92–97	-6.0	-6.6	-1.7	-9.4	-10.8	-9.4	-12.7	-23.5	3.2	-7.4
Panel 4: performance (as Panel 1) weighted by GDP/head										
mean 79–89	-4.7	-7.2	-6.5	-3.4	-14.5	-12.9	-18.1	-37.3	-37.3	-8.5
mean 92–97	-4.3	-5.4	0.1	-8.1	-10.8	-9.2	-10.7	-32.2	6.2	-4.7

Source: European Economy (1998), own calculations – GDP growth, Table 10; inflation, Table 25; unemployment, Table 3; balance of payments, Tables 36 and 40; GDP per head, Table 9. *OECD Employment Outlook* (various years), own calculations – non-employment rate.

Table 3.4b Relative performance in selected countries (comparison with the USA)

	diff US–Au	diff US–Sv	diff US–NL	diff US–Ger	diff US–UK	diff US–Fr	diff US–It	diff US–Sp	diff US–Irl
Panel 1: performance (= growth – unemployment – inflation + trade balance)									
mean 79–89	-7.4	-4.4	-5.7	-8.5	1.9	2.1	6.0	13.9	11.7
mean 92–97	-2.0	-1.4	-6.8	2.1	3.8	3.1	4.4	18.0	-12.7
Panel 2a: performance (= growth – unemployment – inflation)									
mean 79–89	-5.4	-1.4	-0.6	-3.8	4.2	3.9	7.6	15.7	10.2
mean 92–97	-0.6	5.3	0.4	4.1	4.1	6.7	9.2	19.2	2.0
Panel 2b: performance (= growth – non-employment – inflation + trade balance)									
mean 92–97	6.5	-4.0	2.0	9.2	4.5	12.4	21.8	28.5	-0.1
Panel 3a: performance (as Panel 1) with unemployment worse than inflation									
mean 79–89	-9.2	-7.1	-3.7	-8.2	3.2	2.6	5.6	19.0	14.3
mean 92–97	-3.2	1.3	-5.3	3.5	5.4	7.1	7.5	27.1	-4.4
Panel 3b: performance (as Panel 1) with inflation worse than unemployment									
mean 79–89	-7.3	-1.2	-6.6	-8.9	3.2	3.5	10.2	15.6	12.8
mean 92–97	-1.4	-0.8	-5.7	2.1	3.5	2.0	5.3	16.1	-10.6
Panel 4: performance (as Panel 1) weighted by GDP/head									
mean 79–89	-3.8	-1.3	-2.0	-5.1	6.0	4.4	9.6	28.8	28.8
mean 92–97	-0.4	0.7	-4.8	3.4	6.0	4.4	5.9	27.5	-11.0

Source: European Economy (1998), own calculations – GDP growth, Table 10; inflation, Table 25; unemployment, Table 3; balance of payments, Tables 36 and 40; GDP per head, Table 9. *OECD Employment Outlook* (various years), own calculations – non-employment rate.

95

explains much of the improvement shown by France between the two periods.

The second test for sensitivity that was applied was the use of the 'non-employment rate' instead of the unemployment rate in calculating performance scores. The non-employment rate measures the share of the working age population not at work, while the unemployment rate measures the numbers of registered job seekers, but not the inactive, disabled or early retired. The results are shown in Panel 2b.[4] From this the following can be seen.

- Ireland's 'star' performance is dimmed due to high inactivity levels, and Italy's score is also pulled down for the same reasons.
- By contrast, the score for the UK, the USA and Sweden, where (female) participation is much higher, has improved, and each of these outperforms both Germany and Austria.

Performance scores when different priorities are placed on unemployment and inflation (each is weighted in turn to be twice as bad as the other) are shown in Panels 3a and 3b. The effect of using different weights shows the most interesting results when the case of Sweden is considered.

- Sweden does considerably better (its absolute score) in the 1980s than in the 1990s if the measure of performance emphasises keeping down open unemployment (Panel 3a), and considerably better in the 1990s than in the 1980s if the emphasis is put on controlling inflation (Panel 3b). In fact, in the 1980s, there was a high premium in Swedish policymaking on keeping unemployment low, even at the cost of inflation, but in the 1990s, the fight against inflation was given priority and unemployment was allowed to rise.
- In Spain, Italy, France and Ireland, the difference in scores shown in Panels 3a and 3b is much greater in the 1990s than in the 1980s. This reflects the general concern with reducing inflation, to meet the Maastricht convergence criteria.
- The net result of this is that the difference between Austria and Germany, the UK, France, Italy and Spain in the 1990s is relatively small in Panel 3b (where inflation is the greater evil)

compared with the difference shown in Panel 3a (where unemployment is the 'greater evil').

The effect of taking into account a country's wealth is shown in Panel 4. This adjustment has a considerable impact on the score of the USA in the 1980s, when this country was, by a long way, one of the richest in the world. However, of greater interest is the impact of using such a weighting on the once-poor, and on the still-poor, EU countries.

- Ireland's score in the 1980s is pulled down substantially, and this makes its performance in the 1990s, when GDP per head went from being well below the EU average to somewhat above it, yet more impressive.
- Spain, where incomes – while improving – continue to be low, remains the 'least successful' of the countries in the sample.
- Ireland's success might be attributable, in part, to a 'catching up' effect, but Spain, which might have been considered eligible to do the same, did not benefit to anything like the same extent from such an effect.

It is difficult to draw immediate conclusions from the table. Indeed, one of the initial impressions given is that countries that are very different in their institutions and practices have broadly similar scores. Equally, countries which are prima facie similar, and have sometimes been categorised as such in the literature on 'varieties of capitalism' and 'welfare state regimes', perform quite differently.

Referring to one of the country characteristics outlined in Table 1.3 – income inequality – a further highly ambiguous picture is revealed.

- The two countries with the widest income distribution – the USA and the UK – were the two that performed amongst the best if employment rates are taken into account rather than unemployment rates (these are the high employment economies with large low-wage sectors).
- On the other hand, for many years, Sweden maintained a high employment level alongside a much more egalitarian income distribution.
- The two countries showing the most substantial changes in performance – Ireland and the Netherlands – had very different

income distributions. However, in the Netherlands, improvement in performance was associated with a widening in the distribution of income, while in Ireland it was associated with a halt in the narrowing of that distribution.

- Austria experienced a relative stagnation in performance and a slight widening of the income spread, whereas in Germany, where performance declined, this does not appear to have been the case.
- Despite being a poor performer, income distribution in Spain is reasonably egalitarian.

3.5   CONCLUSIONS

Trying to relate performance to 'social partnership/dialogue' approaches and 'social protection' systems, and to their evolution, was of course the ultimate challenge and objective of this analysis. While causality per se cannot be established, certain associations can be identified.

There appear to be three countries that have experienced a relative stagnation of performance or even some decline. These are **Austria**, **Germany** and **Spain**. Austria and Germany are oft-cited examples of neo-corporatism, as demonstrated throughout this book. Austria is a country where there has been little change in the systems of governance and only limited change in the welfare state. Germany, too, has experienced only limited change to date. The difference between the two countries, however, is that there have been some initial movements towards change in the latter. There have been tentative steps toward decentralisation of wage fixing and the setting of rules organising work in Germany and the government has sought to modify important elements of social protection, especially the pension system. None the less, change has encountered considerable resistance.

Spain, which, as a poor country and as one that has benefited from EU fiscal transfers, might have been expected to have benefited from a catch-up effect, has remained a poor performer. However, the country still carries the lingering burden of 'authoritarian corporatism'. Under the Franco régime, labour institutions were hierarchical and unitary and continued to reflect their authoritarian origins despite a certain evolution over the 1960s and 1970s. Despite the gradual modernisation of the country's labour market institutions since the mid-1970s, 'overcoming the legacy of history is not straightforward' and its impact on economic performance still shows (Martínez Lucio, 1998: 455).

Each of these three countries therefore appears to be – though for different reasons – a relatively poor adapter.

There is a second group of countries of which performance has improved over the recent period. These are the Netherlands, Ireland, Sweden, the United Kingdom, the United States and France and Italy. These constitute three distinct sub-groups. In the first sub-group are the **Netherlands, Sweden** and **Ireland**. Each of these countries displays neo-corporatist traits. However, each of them has been moving toward a supply-side corporatism, which places a considerable premium upon decentralisation, ordered deregulation and a respect for the role of markets. The first two countries have also taken substantial steps to modify and adapt their systems of social protection. All three countries have shown a willingness to adapt, and where necessary, to rely upon governments taking radical initiatives, even at the cost of offending the social partners. Each of the three countries has found itself, at one stage or another, 'close to the abyss', and each has found new ways of formulating economic and social policy. In each, the government and the social partners have accepted a redefinition of competence and responsibility.

In the second sub-group are the **United Kingdom** and the **United States**. Throughout the 1980s and 1990s, both were highly market-oriented. The United States has arguably long benefited from a flexible supply side. The United Kingdom had to overcome a weak, and perhaps therefore never particularly efficient, neo-corporatist legacy. In the 1980s and 1990s a market-oriented system was re-established.

In the third group are **France** and **Italy**. These have only limited characteristics in common. The former is statist, while the latter is typified by a weak state. In both cases, questions can be asked about the meaning of the improvement and the extent of success. In both countries, much of it can be attributed to the running of a surplus on the external balance, whilst at the same time experiencing unemployment and non-employment.

Much interest has focused recently on the 'renaissance of neo-corporatism' (for example, Pochet and Fajertag, 1997; Schmitter and Grote, 1997). However, its economic benefits are so far more difficult to assess. It cannot be denied that Ireland's leap forward occurred simultaneously with the establishment of neo-corporatist governance structures. However, Ireland's social partnership shares features of the new supply-side corporatism as much as those of the traditional corporatism found in certain continental European countries. Furthermore, there are some who would argue that the country owed its about turn to external rather than internal factors – that is, to the substantial injections of European Union regional assistance and agricultural support that it enjoyed, rather than any virtuous approach to policy formulation it adopted.

The relatively poorly performing countries of Italy and Spain have sought solutions by entering into negotiations with, and offering deals to, organised capital and labour. So far, it has not been possible to indicate substantial success or failure of their attempts. This is because they are relatively recent and have had insufficient time either to lead to the implementation of actual policies or for those policies that have been implemented to take effect. On the other hand, although many observers had feared they were amongst the candidates for EMU most likely to fail, both of these countries succeeded in meeting the Maastricht convergence criteria. There are certainly some commentators (for example, Pochet, 1998) who would wish to attribute a certain part of this success to their experiments with pacts.

In short, there is some indication here that *traditional* neo-corporatist structures are associated with poorer performance, and that, to survive, structures, even if participatory in some ways, have to adapt. This, if anything, is the first lesson that can be drawn from this analysis. A second lesson is one provoked by the recognition that neo-corporatism is very much associated with small countries, most explicitly by Katzenstein (1985). It is to be noted that the 'successful' countries broke into two groups. One consisted of countries that had adapted neo-corporatist structures, while the other consisted of countries that operated market-based structures with what were often regarded as relatively limited systems of social protection. Those in the first group – Ireland, the Netherlands and Sweden – are small countries, while those in the second group – the United Kingdom and the USA – are large ones. A number of commentators, from very different starting points, have developed reasons to explain why smaller groupings might be more likely to engage in mutually beneficial co-operative behaviour than larger ones. Hardin (1982), for example, shows this with respect to *n*-person, repeated games where it is recognised that acquisition of information about the other players is costly and so such costs tend to fall in smaller communities where there are fewer players. Katzenstein (1985) suggests that since small societies cannot afford to engage in excessive functional specialisation, there is necessarily a close contact between élites.[5] If this is the case, the second group of countries – even if they had regarded it as ideologically acceptable – may not have had the approach of the first group available to them. This means that the route to success has, for them, to be different. In the case of the United Kingdom and the United States this involved non-intervention or deregulation, though it is of course possible to speculate about the desirability of other routes too.

NOTES

1. The Phillips curve is conventionally taken to measure the relationship between changes in wages and (changes in/deviation from trend of) unemployment. Long term and short term relationships can be estimated and the former are normally found to be larger than the latter (for recent estimates, see Sinclair and Horsewood, 1997). The misery index links levels of unemployment to levels of inflation.
2. There are, of course, many other variables which are highly visible and much commented upon but which are not necessary to add into such a summation. One of these is productivity. However, this is better considered as an input variable because high productivity contributes to performance rather than being a component of performance.
3. A rather different benchmark indicator is the Human Development Index produced by the United Nations Development Programme. This effectively adds up scores for life expectancy, literacy and GDP to compare the performance of developing countries. Many of the problems of summation raised above are also discussed by its authors (see UNDP, 1990).
4. The absolute scores are adjusted by subtracting the difference between the unemployment rate and the non-employment rate for the USA from the total that was calculated. The consequence is that the score for the USA is the same in Panel 2b as it is in Panel 1.
5. The reader should note that this does not imply that all small countries are, therefore, successful. Collective action is not necessarily welfare enhancing and 'social capital' can be used for negative as well as positive ends. Austria is a case of a less than entirely successful small country where the incidence of collective action, and the 'social capital quotient', appears to be high.

4 Matters Arising

This book has sought to analyse the changing nature of social partnership and social protection across nine member states of the EU and assess its impact on their economic performance. It has offered a starting point for discussion by proposing definitions of social partnership, dialogue and protection, outlining relevant trends, developing a set of quantitative indicators of performance and seeking to link these to different approaches to policy formulation. In this final chapter, attention is directed to three issues that pertain to the relationship between social partnership and economic performance that have been raised so far. These three issues are, in turn:

- social partnership as a dynamic process;
- the role of EU-level social policy; and
- social partnership as an inclusive process.

The first of these develops certain aspects of the discussion that has run through all three of the previous chapters, since it is about the relationship between institutions and economic outcomes both in theory and in practice. The second issue goes beyond the analysis contained so far in this book as it relates to the extent to which the EU might itself assist the achievement of those conditions identified in Chapter 3 as conducive to successful performance. Over recent years the EU has increasingly stressed the contribution of social partnership to social policy, and the practicalities of this approach are explored. The third issue arises from the debate about how appropriate social partnership is as a means of formulating economic and social policy and asks how, both in individual member states and across the EU as a whole, its representativity might be improved and expanded.

4.1 SOCIAL PARTNERSHIP AS A DYNAMIC PROCESS

The first matter arising focuses primarily on certain of the concepts and approaches implicit in this study. An understanding of the contribution of social partnership/dialogue and social protection to economic performance requires an understanding of their dynamic, changing nature. In particular, it requires full account to be taken of the forms that prevailing institutions might adopt, as well as sensitivity to the assumptions made and the validity of the outcome measures that are used.

Complexity of Social Partnership

This study has highlighted the complexities that lurk behind the term social partnership by indicating the range of dimensions that it covers. These include methods, levels, forms and subject areas for social partnership as well as the extent of their formality or informality. Analysis across countries shows that emphasis on any one of these dimensions is likely to lead to a skewed understanding of the realities of participation in any given country. For example, concentration on intersectoral levels of social partnership risks underestimating the significance of pressures to decentralise influence to sector or company level. The study also shows how all these dimensions react together in a dynamic way, and how what is emphasised is subject to evolutionary processes. Social partnership may become increasingly decentralised, it may become more advisory than consultative and its legal basis may come under question. One reason for such changes is that its contribution to economic performance is kept under continual review by governments, employers and unions. In those countries, such as Austria, where the structure of such dialogue, for whatever reason, is seen as largely unproblematic, there is little pressure for change. In most other countries, however, social partnership has been adapted – according to the circumstances, to a greater or lesser extent. The analysis illustrates moves towards more advisory methods in countries such as the Netherlands and Sweden, but a strengthening of consultative methods, particularly at intersectoral level, in other countries, such as Ireland, Italy and Spain.

However, the analysis also reveals that 'continuums of participation'

(Blyton and Turnbull, 1998) can contrast with one another at different levels of the economy. With respect to industrial relations, continuums of participation range from information disclosure at one end, through consultation and negotiation, to workers' control at the other end. Many factors determine the location of the 'frontier of control' (Goodrich, 1975) at any one moment, including management style, trade union densities, the stage of the economic cycle and the political complexion of the government. Indeed, investigation shows that, in general, the influence of tripartite, intersectoral forums for dialogue has been downgraded in EU member states in recent years. In the same way, sector-level bargaining over pay and conditions has come under pressure, and responsibility has been decentralised to company or workplace level.

However, the loss, or downgrading, of social partnership at higher levels may be compensated by its gain, or revitalisation, at lower levels. Decentralisation, as outlined in Chapter 2, may take place in a more or less organised manner. Broad policy frameworks agreed by the social partners at central or sectoral levels may be complemented by the negotiation of the detail by their counterparts at company or workplace levels, in a process of organised decentralisation. In Germany and the Netherlands, for example, decentralisation has meant greater influence for works councillors at company or workplace over pay levels through the operation of 'opening clauses'. Trade union structures in Italy have been reformed to allow greater co-ordination of bargaining between sectoral and company or workplace levels. New forms of employee representation have been introduced in France and the UK specifically to promote social dialogue in workplaces where it may otherwise be lacking. In France, a member of staff may be delegated expressly to negotiate on pay and working time, whilst in the UK – generally cited as an example of disorganised decentralisation (Traxler, 1995a: 6–7) – special provisions for employee representation in non-unionised workplaces had to be introduced in 1994 to comply with EU consultation requirements in cases of redundancy.

These developments reveal the multidirectional and multidimensional nature of social partnership – that is, the way in which movements towards weaker forms at one level may be accompanied by movements towards stronger forms at another. Analysis has also demonstrated the cyclical nature of social partnership. The original impetus for national understandings in Ireland occurred in the late

1970s, though eventual success was not achieved until the changed conditions of the 1980s. In the UK, the new Labour government has promoted what it terms 'new forms of social partnership at work' – by which reference is made to legislation on union recognition rights and a minimum wage – thus putting a brake on almost 20 years of government emphasis on managerial prerogative. The German unions proposed a tripartite Alliance for Jobs, the formulation of which implies procedures not unreminiscent of the concerted action that was tried in the late 1960s and early 1970s, and the newly-elected German government held the first tripartite talks in December 1998. In Spain, the government has restarted a process of intersectoral bargaining in an attempt to reform creaking industrial relations structures, despite the failure of such an approach in the mid-1980s.

These cyclical pressures on the institutions of social partnership may give a sense of fragility or ephemerality to the processes involved. Put another way, 'the protagonists' *willingness* to conclude social pacts' may contrast with their '*capacity* to conclude social pacts' which is dependent on 'a favourable structural framework' (Traxler, 1997: 33 [emphasis in original]).

Ireland provides an example of such fragility. There the system of national understandings requires ratification by each of the unions affiliated to the central confederation of trade unions. Any failure to ratify would nullify the entire intersectoral agreement, as the confederation is not empowered to impose it on its members. Another instance may be found in Italy, where the intersectoral agreements are vulnerable to changes in government, since alternative coalitions in parliament might not be prepared to deliver the government's side of the bargain.

The ephemerality of some processes stems from the fact that many developments in social partnership have their origins as a reaction to crisis – either economic or political. As Pochet and Fajertag (1997: 12) indicate in relation to social pacts: 'With the exception of Germany, these social pacts were preceded by an *impasse* in industrial relations, together with stormy relations between the government and social partners.' The Irish and Italian cases are examples of this, but developments in Spain, Sweden and the Netherlands also illustrate the point. In Ireland, Italy and Spain, tripartite pacts provided the framework for reform of a range of areas, ranging from industrial relations to social security and training. By contrast, in the Netherlands, the social partners avoided the threat of a government-imposed freeze on wages and prices by reaching their own bipartite agreement on pay and employment. In Sweden, the employers pulled out of a number of tripartite bodies to gain greater independence for themselves. Each of these countries' experience represents a pragmatic or opportunistic response to pressure that demonstrates cycles of influence as much as any steady progress towards social partnership as a valued principle of policy formulation in its own right.

How well such fragile and ephemeral processes survive and become embedded depends upon the benefits they are perceived to bring, and these perceived benefits are likely to depend as much on external events as on the results the partnership processes themselves produce. Analysts of the Dutch experience talk of the country being blessed by *fortuna* as well as by *virtu* (Visser and Hemmerijk, 1997, quoting Machiavelli), and of the Irish experience as a consequence of 'good luck' and 'good timing' as well as 'good policies' (Krugman, 1997).

Social pacts, which arguably contribute to desirable outcomes, may also have procedural outcomes which some would defend in their own right. They confer legitimacy and/or strengthen the status of organisations of employees at a time when, in many countries, union membership is in decline and when political and economic philosophy has been giving increasing primacy to the individual. However, at the same time as conferring legitimacy, they also place limits on the competence of the participating actors. In the case of Ireland and the Netherlands, the trade unions entered the process of making central agreements from a point of relative weakness and rising levels of unemployment. They gained 'voice' in certain areas, but had to accept that the government had the right to dictate policy in other areas. However, employers, too, had to make concessions. They had to grant voice, and this meant that they had to be prepared to discuss certain issues that they might have preferred not to discuss. On occasions, both parties had an interest in making an agreement with each other if the alternative was a settlement imposed by government.

Employers and unions might well be prepared to try and reach an intersectoral accord if the alternative is government interference in the wage-fixing process, and this in turn explains why social partnership is particularly intimately related to matters of industrial relations. It also suggests that some, if not many, of the arrangements described in this study are cases of organisations or actors trying to 'regain power by sharing it' (Flanders, 1967: 32). In other words, certain concessions are made to ensure that other rights or powers are respected or reinforced. Governments, as well as employers and unions, have such a strategy. This book has illustrated this, particularly by pointing to examples of governments that seek to implement social security reforms – trading off the right to take action in this area through granting relative autonomy to the social partners in other areas.

Assessing the Impact of Social Partnership

The specificity of the experiences described and analysed in this book have underlined the problems and pitfalls that are necessarily encountered in any attempt to draw up typologies of institutions and governance. Theorists may agree that the role of institutions is critical in determining economic performance, but they differ widely over *which* institutions are central – forms of welfare provision, corporate governance or labour market regulation – and then over *which* countries fit into the typologies that they have drawn up. There is, for example, debate over whether Germany can be described as a 'concerted economy', or whether Italy and Spain should be described as 'statist' or as 'network/clan societies' (Van Waarden, 1997). Equally, there is the question of subsystems and how they interrelate. For example, although the social welfare systems of France and Germany are frequently described as similar (Gough, 1996), their systems of corporate governance are quite distinct, which makes it difficult to know how one should insert these two countries into a schema of 'varieties of capitalism'. Furthermore, there is the risk that concentration on drawing up typologies leads to an oversimplified view of developments. There is the tendency to talk in terms of a limited number of alternatives – on the one side neo-corporatist or 'concertation' models and on the other neo-liberal or free market models (Crouch, 1995; Traxler, 1997). Such polarised approaches may risk overlooking subtleties in national institutional arrangements and dynamics.

This book has argued, rather, that countries cannot be forced into neatly theorised models – however alluring or reassuring they may appear – any more than a child can solve a Rubik's cube puzzle by wrenching each of its elements into a position to produce the desired result of six sides each of a single colour.

In practice, a preoccupation with typologies often degenerates into a sterile debate on taxonomy rather than producing answers to the more interesting question of how institutional arrangements affect performance. It was because the latter was the objective of this analysis that individual nation states were chosen as the unit of investigation in an attempt to bypass such digressions. Furthermore, one of the most striking points to emerge from this analysis has been the diversity of policy formulation processes with respect to economic, industrial relations, training and social security issues that can be found in something as relatively homogeneous as the EU area. This point is picked up again in the final section on social partnership as an inclusive process.

To allow comparison between the selected countries, a number of simple indicators of economic performance were developed. Using these, certain conclusions were drawn. In particular, the study suggested that traditional neo-corporatist structures tended to be associated with 'poorer' performance and that participatory structures and social welfare provision – to survive – have to adapt in the ways outlined above. However, two points must be stressed.

First, in considering the links between institutions and outcomes, the question of causality is by no means always clear. The study points out that although the presence of social partnership might correlate with good performance, this could be because partnership leads to consensus and stability, or because other factors induce good performance and good performance creates the surpluses required to permit partnership.

Second, the notion of economic performance that this book employs is highly restricted. It refers to a number of standard economic indicators such as growth, inflation, unemployment and the external balance. However, these indicators do not measure many wider aspects of welfare or take into account externalities, such as environmental pollution or rising levels of social inequality and exclusion. It is perfectly legitimate to argue that democratic and participatory forms of governance – perhaps, even, 'psychological well-being' – are ends in themselves, and that they should not be assessed instrumentally in relation to their impact on growth or inflation. That is, people may wish to trade off more rigorous forms of social partnership against lower growth rates because they believe that it is, in itself, a social good. They may not wish market forces in their brute form to act as arbiter of employment and social policy.

4.2 ROLE OF EU-LEVEL SOCIAL POLICY

The second matter arising relates to the two propositions suggested at the end of Chapter 3. One is that flexibility and adaptability can improve a country's economic performance with respect to a range of indicators including growth and inflation and, above all, employment. The other is that social partnership can play a significant role in consolidating the social structures required to secure the flexibility and adaptability that enables successful performance to be achieved. This section discusses current EU policies which seek to promote higher employment in this light. The section begins by examining the background to EU social policy and tracing the way it has become increasingly concerned with countering unemployment. It then looks in more detail at two aspects of what is sometimes referred to as the European Employment Strategy, the issuing of employment policy guidelines to member states and the agreement on a European Employment Pact.

From Workers' Rights to Employment Promotion

The framers of the founding and subsequent Treaties of the European Union (EU)[1] have always recognised that closer economic integration amongst the member states could lead to a deterioration in employment conditions. This was seen as a consequence of:

- initially, an increase in cross-border trade leading to pressure by employers to reduce labour costs and employment rights to the lowest common denominator (social dumping);
- subsequently, and with the further removal of tariff barriers and other impediments to trade, structural changes in member state economies that could create job losses; and
- more recently, especially in the light of the Maastricht convergence criteria, pressures on public expenditure, cuts in social security and welfare state provision.

Nevertheless, the general tone of the Treaty of Rome (1957) with respect to social policy has been described as 'neo-liberal' (Hepple, 1987: 77). In other words, it was generally assumed that market forces, operating through the common market and assisted by the provisions of the Treaty itself, would 'favour the harmonisation of social systems' (Article 117). The Treaty itself spoke merely of a requirement that member states would co-operate across a variety of 'social fields' that included employment, labour law and working conditions, vocational training, social security, health and safety at work, collective bargaining and rights of association.

However, controversy centred from the beginning on how far harmonisation should proceed and in which areas, and how narrowly or broadly the notion of social policy should be construed. It was argued, for example, in the 1950s that a more interventionist approach should be developed to counteract distortions to competition resulting from labour legislation or social security schemes that were more favourable to workers in one country than in another. However, it was eventually agreed amongst the original signatories of the Treaty that only specific distortions should be considered. This led to Articles 119 and 120, protecting equal pay and holiday pay, that were included at the behest of France, which feared that its more generous provisions in these areas would lead to competitive disadvantage for its employers. To complement the objective of a free market in goods, the Treaty also sought to ensure the free movement of workers and, in accordance with this, regulated their rights under national social security systems. It also set up the European Structural Funds to assist the less-developed regions, including the European Social Fund to assist in vocational training.

Amendments since the mid-1980s have substantially extended the competence of the Commission and the Council. The Single European Act, for example, established a legal basis in the Treaty for the process of 'social dialogue' between European level organisations representing employers and unions with respect both to matters affecting pan-EU labour affairs and to matters affecting particular sectors at EU level. Social dialogue not only gave the social partners access to policy formulation but it also gave them, at least potentially, responsibility for policy implementation through collective bargaining and consultation at sector, company or workplace levels to insert the detail agreed at EU level. The Maastricht Treaty extended qualified majority voting in the Council to a wide range of social policy areas (although until 1997 the UK opted out of these provisions, which were contained in a separate 'social protocol'). The Amsterdam Treaty, as detailed below, consolidated a shift in EU social policy towards employment promotion.

Nevertheless, there have continued to be fundamental political divergences between those who advocate the greater regulation of employment and social affairs at EU level and those who want little more than a free trade area. This lack of consensus over what was either desirable or achievable reflected, in part, the range of institutional settings across the member states themselves. In the 1980s, the Conservative UK government advocated the same free market policies for the EU that it had adopted at the domestic level, but the Christian Democrat German government, accustomed to a more interventionist stance in its social policy, was much more sympathetic to regulation. The accession of three new member states in 1995 – Austria, Finland and Sweden – each with historically low levels of unemployment, and each with its own variant of social partnership – no doubt contributed to a shift of emphasis in what might be expected or achievable. So, too, did subsequent changes in political complexion of member state governments – in the UK (1997), in France (1997) and in Germany (1998). However, structural factors were important, too, in particular the development of the Single European Market (SEM), which deepened concerns over rising levels of unemployment, and the prospect of European Monetary Union.

The 1992 Maastricht Treaty was, with hindsight, to mark the high-water level of the interventionist approach to workers' rights. Thereafter employment promotion came increasingly to the fore. The Commission's 1993 White Paper on growth, competitiveness and employment stressed the role of training, flexibility and work reorganisation in reducing the level of unemployment across the EU (Commission, 1993). The Essen summit of 1994 emphasised the fight against unemployment as the main task of social policy. It followed the prescriptions of the White Paper but added reference to measures that increased the job intensity of growth and reduced non-wage labour costs and called on member states to give greater weight to active labour market policies and to target groups particularly hard hit by unemployment (Commission, 1994b). The Amsterdam summit of 1997, drawing upon these concerns, resulted in agreement to insert an 'employment chapter' into the Treaty governing the principles of the Union. Article 2 of the Treaty of Amsterdam made for the first time 'a high level of employment' an objective of the EU and required member states to regard its achievement as a matter of common interest. The Treaty authorised the Council to draw up guidelines which member governments should respect when drawing up policies to meet the objectives it had set.

Employment Guidelines and the National Action Plans

The first set of such guidelines was approved at the Luxembourg 'jobs summit' at the end of 1997. For 1999 new guidelines, containing minor revisions, were issued. The guidelines require each member state to submit a National Action Plan on employment (NAP) every year, in a standard format, under four common 'pillars' concerned, respectively, with improving 'employability'; developing entrepreneurship; encouraging adaptability in businesses and their employees; and strengthening policies for equal opportunities. Critically, the guidelines reserve a central role for the social partners. They consolidate the developing part to be played by employers and unions in the development of employment regulation at EU level by specifying that 'the social partners at all levels will be involved in all stages of this approach and will make an important contribution to the implementation of these guidelines and a high level of employment. That contribution will be regularly assessed' (Commission, 1997c: para. 9).

Although the individual NAPs represent the respective national governments' assessments of how the formulation of policy proceeded, certain patterns emerge as expected. Thus, the Swedish NAP declares that the 'social partners have significant responsibility for employment policy' and that 'a tradition of co-operation between responsible social partners' has contributed to the country's flexible, decentralised system of work organisation (Commission, 1998a: 9). In a similar fashion, the Austrian NAP refers to its 'long and successful tradition of co-operation' (Commission, 1998a: 10) and the Dutch NAP to the creation in the Netherlands of 'a confidence-building economy' through social partnership (Commission, 1998a: 10). The NAPs of Austria and Ireland, and of the UK, where discourse about partnership had reasserted itself, contained text that was agreed with, or even jointly drafted by, the principal organisations representing business and employees. With respect to the subject matter of consultation, most governments suggested that this had taken place around the issues of training and lifelong learning – the subject of the 'employability' pillar – and modernising work organisation – the subject of the 'encouraging adaptability' pillar. This is scarcely surprising, since these are the areas where both employers and unions can and do have a direct influence upon practice.

However, it also has to be recognised that the extent of consultation and harmony was not always as great as the NAPs themselves suggest, or the Commission's initial assessment of them (Commission, 1998f), maintains. In some cases, such as in Austria, Germany, Sweden and Italy, the social partners were happy enough with the consultation process, but expressed criticism over the actual outcome of the NAP. In other cases, notably in France and Spain, the social partners were also upset over what they viewed as altogether inadequate consultation. Sometimes these divergences were serious. The German government, for example, presented its NAP in April 1998, following several rounds of talks with the social partners covering general economic policy, social and labour market policy and vocational training policy. However, none of the rounds of talks resulted in the issuing of a joint statement or recommendation. Indeed, the German trade union federation (DGB) called the final NAP 'all in all disappointing' and in some points a 'provocation' (such as the government's presentation of cuts in sickness benefit or the weakening of dismissal legislation as employment promotion). Meanwhile, the employers expressed scepticism that governments could do much to create jobs and argued that the best employment policy was one promoting profitable investment and reducing taxes and labour costs (EIRO, DE9805263F). This was reminiscent of the failures in previous years of round table meetings and attempts to establish an 'Alliance for Jobs'.

In France, where the social partnership tradition was weak, the consultation that did occur was criticised as too brief and too insubstantial. One of the major union confederations noted that whilst two discussion meetings had taken place, the NAP had been actually drawn up in interministerial meetings. Although its conclusion of the process was 'disappointing', another of the confederations observed that 'given the tradition of French trade unionism, it is difficult to consider co-operation between various unions and employers in the drawing up of a common plan'. The employers' organisation concurred, stating that the NAP was 'a government plan which did not reflect the social partners' views' (EIRO, FR9805107F). In Spain, the government submitted its NAP to widespread consultation with regional governments, councils, employers, unions and non-governmental organisations, but the two principal union confederations issued a joint statement condemning the NAP for failing to commit public funding to create jobs and for not proposing a statutory reduction in the working week. They went so far as to organise a series of protests and a major rally against the NAP (EIRO, ES9804253N; ES9805152F). The unions' concerns focused not so much on the failure of the government to consult as on its failure to pay any attention to the results of the consultations, but the antagonism reflects the precarious nature of the social partnership tradition in Spain and mirrors past failures to achieve consensus on major issues of economic and social policy.

The European Employment Pact

The Luxembourg jobs summit, although best remembered for the subsequent publication of the guidelines that aimed to improve the ability of individuals to find and hold jobs, made wider statements about the means to achieve the objectives of the Amsterdam Treaty. Employment promotion was recognised as also the consequence of well-coordinated macroeconomic policies and the further development of the internal market. The latter had been the object of attention under the UK presidency in the second half of 1997, which had followed the Dutch presidency and continued to emphasise the virtues of deregulation (though it had also signed the social chapter). In the concluding statement, the Council had committed itself to the pursuit of comprehensive structural reform and modernisation to improve the innovative capacity and efficiency of the labour market and the markets in goods, services and capital. The former was the subject matter of the presidencies of late 1998 and early 1999.

In the general election campaign in Germany, the then opposition Social Democratic Party (SPD) made repeated reference to the need for a European Employment Pact and, having won, included such a commitment in the coalition agreement. The nature of its proposed pact was vague, but the implication was that it could involve co-ordinated expansion by the member states and European-wide infrastructural investment. Discussions under the Austrian and German presidencies refined some of the detail. A critical component of the conception was that growth-oriented macroeconomic policies required stability- and productivity-oriented wages policies. Accordingly, the social partners were seen to have a critical role, but so too were other institutions, including the central banks. A stability- and productivity-oriented wages policy was not taken to mean there would be a collective agreement at European level but 'rather a form of concertation, where every actor takes their own responsibility for engaging in dialogue with others' (Larsson, 1999).

Reference to wages policy was not new. The 'resolution on growth and employment' agreed at the Amsterdam summit had stressed the responsibility of the social partners for reconciling high employment with appropriate wage settlements and for setting up a suitable institutional framework for the wage formation process. The notion of an 'employment friendly' wages policy, whereby

- nominal wage increases were to be consistent with price stability;
- real wages were to be linked to productivity growth; and
- earnings were adequately to reflect the need to maintain or increase the profitability of investment, differences in productivity and regional circumstances

had been repeated in successive guidelines on economic policy endorsed by the Council. However, there had been criticisms, which were beginning to be recognised at EU level, that there was insufficient synergy between these annual Broad Economic Policy Guidelines and the recently agreed Employment Guidelines (Commission, 1999a). The European Employment Pact, as it came to be developed under the German presidency, can be seen as an attempt to overcome this. However, emphasis on the promotion of growth as such was diluted, and emphasis on stability, as a precursor to growth, came to the fore. This reflected a shift in emphasis in Germany itself as marked by the sudden resignation of the 'Keynesian' finance minister, as well as a lack of enthusiasm in other member countries.

The pact that was endorsed at the Cologne Council in June 1999 reiterated that the fight against unemployment was 'the most important objective of [Europe's] economic and social policy'. It effectively repeated the Amsterdam principles of higher employment being contingent upon underlying macroeconomic conditions, on the quality of the labour force and on competitive markets. What it added was a process to help achieve the first of these three requirements, namely a Macroeconomic Dialogue, that would involve economic and finance ministers and social affairs ministers, the Commission itself, the central bank and the social partners. The responsibility of this dialogue would be to ensure mutually supportive interaction between wage developments, fiscal policy and monetary policy.

Although criticised as contributing little new to European social policy, and as merely repackaging existing commitments and sentiments, the pact does have two novel features. First, it represents an acknowledgement that employment could not be dealt with separately from other issues of economic and social policy. The Luxembourg process, by compartmentalising labour market policy, could be seen as implying that such compartmentalisation was indeed possible. The Employment Pact, by linking in the broad economic guidelines with their concern for budget consolidation, social security reform and labour market deregulation, implies that, potentially, each is a subject for social dialogue. Second, it emphasises that wages policy is a critical component of employment policy. The Luxembourg summit had scarcely touched upon this and the guidelines that were issued were not concerned with it at all. At the same time, the pronouncements of economics and finance ministers had traditionally been couched in terms of growth or inflation performance rather than employment performance. One of the commitments of the pact was the establishment of a biannual forum in which the various parties could exchange views and assess the implications of agreed and comprehensive background information.

Looked at in this way, the pact appears to draw heavily from the specific experiences of particular member states. The Austrian example springs immediately to mind, as does the German experiment with concerted action. On the other hand, the background documentation makes expected references to 'subsidiarity', in that it stresses that the task of creating conditions for more employment and growth 'is primarily a matter for member states' (Presidency, 1999). Moreover, it makes explicit mention of how this applies with respect to the wage formation process. The autonomy of the social partners in collective bargaining is underlined, and differences in systems of wage determination and the levels at which this determination occurs are acknowledged. In this respect, the pact is compatible with principles of flexibility and decentralisation that have been identified as components of success.

4.3 SOCIAL PARTNERSHIP AS AN INCLUSIVE PROCESS

The third matter arising has its origins in the debate about how democratic the social partnership process is. This raises questions about who is represented in decisions about public policy and how. Partnership that involves only organised capital and organised labour bypasses many important social interests – such as the unemployed, pensioners and consumers – and might also usurp the place of democratically elected government. This section considers the extent to which different forms of social partnership can be considered to add authority to policy making and goes on to consider ways in which its legitimacy and effectiveness might be improved. Considerable attention is paid to the European dimension of social partnership, but examples are also drawn from individual countries included in the study.

Social Partnership and the Democratic Deficit

This book has stressed that social partnership has intrinsic as well as extrinsic value. It is seen as providing for a greater degree of involvement in policy that both enhances the quality of decisions taken and encourages adherence to them by the bodies affected. Traditionally, participation in the formulation of economic and social policy has been analysed with respect to its occurrence in two spheres – the political sphere and the workplace sphere.

In the first of these spheres, political parties compete to present economic and social programmes that will attract the public at election time. Institutional and legal frameworks protect a variety of freedoms, including the right to vote, that are exercised by citizens to safeguard or advance their interests. The countries in this study generally keep these frameworks under review to ensure that they remain fair and efficient. In recent years, for example, France and Italy have reformed their electoral systems whilst Spain and the UK have devolved measures of political power to their regions.

In the second sphere, employers, trade unions and works councils cooperate through various forms of employee participation procedures. In the countries covered by this study, the immediate distribution of income that the collaboration of capital and labour has produced is negotiated between employers and trade unions. Depending upon the country, issues of work organisation, performance and matters concerning individual employees are dealt with by works councils, trade unions, joint committees or some other body. Both collective and individual rights and obligations are guaranteed by law and/or enshrined in custom and practice and together these frameworks create a degree of industrial citizenship that contrasts with the political citizenship described above. Moreover, and as this book has shown, in the same way that governments review and adapt the framework of political citizenship, so too do they review and adapt the framework of industrial citizenship.

The creation of the Single European Market and the arrival of European Monetary Union have revealed serious shortcomings in both these participatory spheres at European level – shortcomings that are frequently referred to as the 'democratic deficit'. Successive stages of European economic integration have not been accompanied by an equivalent transition towards a complementary system of European-level democracy either with respect to political involvement or with respect to employee participation. There remain serious deficiencies in the way in which the Commission, which initiates and monitors the implementation of legislation, is made accountable to the elected European Parliament. The powers of the European Parliament are constrained by its inability to propose legislation. The Economic and Social Committee has a restricted, consultative role. The Council of Ministers, broadly speaking the decision maker, is only indirectly accountable to the European electorate through national legislatures. Furthermore, the Commission and the Council normally deliberate in secret. Nevertheless, many of the decisions that make their way through these bodies are binding and highly significant for many millions of people.

Progress in relation to EU-level social dialogue has arguably been greater in recent years than progress in relation to political activity. The social chapter has now been integrated into the text of the Treaty of Amsterdam, and four EU-level collective agreements – on parental leave, part-time work, the working time of seafarers and fixed-term contracts – have been adopted as directives. At the national level, and to a greater or lesser extent, employers and unions have made contributions to the formulation of the National Action Plans for employment. At sector level, social dialogue was active across 23 EU-level industries by 1997, with 40 joint texts adopted that year alone (Commission, 1998c: 12). And at company level, it is estimated that around 550 multinationals have now set up their own European works councils (*European Works Councils Bulletin*, 1999: 10). Nevertheless major challenges remain, especially in the context of the development of European Monetary Union. One is the question of representation and which EU-level social partners are to be officially recognised for the process of social dialogue. Another focuses on the problem of enforce-ability of EU-level agreements, since legal régimes and compliance systems vary widely across the member states. Yet another concerns the prospects for EU-level collective bargaining – whether bargaining may be integrated or co-ordinated across member states and, if so, at which level and covering which topics. The Commission, acknowl-edging the importance of dealing with these issues, has set itself three objectives: 'a more open social dialogue', 'a more effective dialogue between the European institutions and the social partners' and 'the development of a real collective bargaining at European level' (Commission, 1998b: 4).

Until these issues are fully addressed, citizens and workers across the EU are often confronted directly by EU-level decision-making powers without the benefit of those intermediary structures – political parties, unions, interest groups – through which they can seek direct involvement. As a result apathy about the EU is potentially built into the system.

Three Categories of Social Partnership/Dialogue

Three categories of social partnership and dialogue may be distinguished.

1. Forums where employers, workers and their representative bodies (referred to in short as 'insiders') discuss 'insider issues' (such as pay, terms and conditions and rights at work) through consultation procedures and collective bargaining. This may be called 'narrow insider' social dialogue.
2. Forums where insiders also discuss 'outsider' issues (such as job creation measures and employment plans), thus allowing those active in the labour market to engage in the interests of those who are not (outsiders, such as the unemployed, pensioners,

school leavers and the disabled). This may be called 'broad insider' social dialogue.

3. Forums where both insiders and outsiders discuss labour market-oriented issues of joint concern. In such forums, representatives of young people, the unemployed, pensioners, consumer and environmental groups amongst others participate alongside representatives of employed workers and employers. This may be called 'augmented' social dialogue.

Figure 4.1 summarises these three categories of partnership and dialogue.

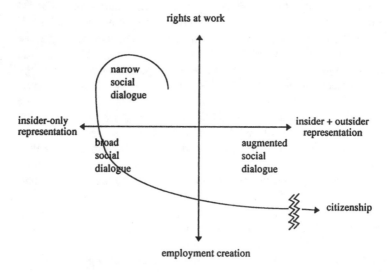

Figure 4.1   Relationships between forms of social dialogue

'Narrow insider' social dialogue

At each stage of EU development, the introduction and expansion of social provisions have accompanied economic integration. For example, the EEC Treaty enshrined the principle of equal pay for equal work (Article 119), the Single European Market programme was complemented by the adoption of the Social Charter and the decision to proceed with EMU was matched by the adoption of the social protocol (since 1997 the social chapter). The rationale for these provisions has been that they assist in promoting the free movement of labour across the member states and in preventing social dumping. That is, they ensure that member states are not involved in a 'race downwards' to undermine working conditions in an attempt to preserve their own competitive advantage. However, others have seen the 'social dimension' as an end in itself – that is, as a way to demonstrate the benefits of the EU to the labour movement and workers in general. Many directives – in areas like equal opportunities, health and safety, collective redundancies and working time – have helped to improve rights at work. In addition, the social dialogue process, as inaugurated by Jacques Delors in 1985, was intended as a way to give the social partners a stake in the creation of 'social Europe', first at intersectoral and sectoral levels and later, through the European works councils directive, at company level too (Carley, 1993; Gold, 1998).

'Broad insider' social dialogue
Under the terms of the employment chapter of the Amsterdam Treaty, the social partners in each of the member states are to be involved in the drawing up and implementation of the National Action Plans. Accordingly, they are now *required* to consider employment issues on an annual basis and to take account of outsider issues as well as the more familiar insider issues. The provisions of the European Employment Pact extend the subject matter of dialogue yet further. By putting wages for the first time at the centre, they again aim to make negotiators more aware of the wider implications of their actions. Yet although such an extension might appear to be an innovation it is in fact a logical continuation of existing trends. The introduction of a single currency has meant that the individual member states of the EU have already been shorn of many of the instruments by which they can affect competitiveness and employment. They are no longer able to make use, by themselves, of interest rate or exchange rate policies. Equally, their scope to use fiscal policy for deficit financing was restricted by the Maastricht convergence criteria, which demand a balanced budget in the medium term and limit national government deficits to 3 per cent in any one year. Meanwhile, the scope for inter-member state transfers is limited by the small size of the structural funds. Since labour mobility between member states is low, the main vehicle for ensuring that employment levels are high is labour market policy itself. One element

of this has to be the restraint of unit labour costs. This requires member states to act upon workforce flexibility and skills, which was the subject matter of the Luxembourg process, but also on wage levels.

'Augmented' social dialogue

Much of the social dialogue discussed so far has been of the narrower, labour market-oriented form outlined above as conducted by insiders. That is, it focuses on the representative abilities of specifically labour market actors, namely employers and unions in the private and public sectors. Broader social partnership occurs in so far as these actors concern themselves with issues such as pensions and labour market policy, and in so far as their organisations regard themselves as, or act as, inclusive bodies.

Formal inclusion of other interest groups is much rarer at national levels within the EU member states. In Austria, social partnership arrangements make no direct provision for consumer interests, although the Chambers of Labour have consumer representation as one of their tasks. In addition, foreign workers, who make up nearly a tenth of the labour force, are ineligible for election to works councils and consequently to positions within the trade unions because most trade unions in Austria set membership of a works council as first step to election to union office. In other countries, such as Italy and Spain, there is no formal representation of any of these groups in social dialogue institutions either, although the Italian unions do have special sections for their retired members. In France, the social partners have been wary of including other groups within social dialogue processes. The unions run their own consumer groups but only one of the five main central confederations (CGT) has its own organisation for the unemployed. However, the French unions have refused to allow other groups for the unemployed representation on the administrative boards of the unemployment benefit funds. This is because they maintain that they represent all workers, whether employed or unemployed.

The most comprehensive form of 'augmented' social dialogue amongst the countries included in this study is Ireland. There, a National Economic and Social Forum (NESF) has been created to represent three sets of interests: government and parliament; employers, unions and agriculture; and women, youth, the unemployed, the disadvantaged, the disabled, the elderly and environmental interests. The NESF has issued reports on a range of economic and social issues such as local development, social welfare and job creation. Initially it fulfilled only an advisory role, but it also took part in the preliminary discussions for Partnership 2000, the social pact on economic and social policy covering the years 1997–2001. However, the central pay agreement, which forms the linchpin of this pact, remains the responsibility of the organisations representing employers and employees.

At EU level, the Economic and Social Committee (ESC) is the body that most nearly approximates an augmented forum. It brings together members from 'the various categories of economic and social activity' (Article 193 of the EEC Treaty) under three categories: employers, unions and other interests (that are drawn from agriculture, consumers, the professions and small- and medium-sized enterprises, amongst others). However, members sit as individuals and not as representatives of their organisations, and so the ESC is seen more as an advisory or consultative forum than as part of the social dialogue process. The Maastricht Treaty contained a declaration stressing the importance of co-operation between the Commission and non-government organisations active in social policy matters. So far, exchanges have been ad hoc and, despite the aspirations of the voluntary sector, no provision for 'civil dialogue' was included in the Amsterdam Treaty (Carley, 1999: 7–8).

Social partnership – whether it is narrow insider, broad insider or the less usual augmented form – has been praised by many. Indeed, at the EU level it might be argued that such forms of dialogue and partnership have the potential to overcome national differences. The participating actors do not represent individual member states but rather broad social groups. Negotiation between countries is replaced by negotiation between classes. More pragmatically, many politicians will share the view of Wim Kok, former leader of the major union federation in the Netherlands, subsequently finance minister and more recently prime minister. He was also one of the signatories of the first of the inter-sectoral accords that arguably contributed to that country's successful performance in the 1990s. According to him, 'any cabinet will have to recognise the reality that, as a government, you want to do a lot, but if you sit down and discuss with the social partners you can do a lot more' (*SER Bulletin*, 1997: 7).

On the other hand, it has to be recognised that, even in the Netherlands, not everyone shared Kok's view. Some Dutch politicians have warned of the 'quicksand of the negotiation-economy', and others have spoken of the need to retreat from corporatism and restore the primacy of politics. Hans Wijers, a minister in the governing coalition till 1998, has argued that 'politicians are responsible for that vague, but nonetheless important, concept of the public interest, and that responsibility cannot ever, repeat ever, be placed in the hands of interest organisations which, by definition, represent only a part of society. That is a question of democracy. Politics should be subject to parliamentary control. Voters can reject politicians. They cannot do the same with institutions' *(SER Bulletin,* 1997: 14).

In the same way, some commentators criticised proposals for an employment pact in Germany – since agreed in December 1998 – as an attempt to resurrect corporatism, rather than as a means to encourage markets, and to divert political decision making away from parliament into the hands of interest groups (Bertold and Fehn, 1996; Hank, 1996; Lang and Kuhlmann, 1996). Similarly despite its use of the term social partnership, the government in the UK, as well as the trade unions, are often at pains to repeat that the process does not involve the handing over of policy making and execution to the unions or employers' associations, and that responsibility remains with the elected government (Taylor, 1998a; 1998b).

The potentially undemocratic nature of certain forms of social dialogue suggests the need to give greater attention to the links between economic participation, social exclusion and citizenship. Expanding the representativity of social dialogue and partnership would enhance the development of the notion of 'EU citizenship'. This is because citizenship is the element that integrates into social life those excluded from the labour market. Citizenship therefore becomes a key concept in ensuring the inclusion of the socially excluded into those social, political and cultural institutions and patterns of life that sustain acceptance and well-being (García, 1992).

However, citizenship of the EU is still defined primarily by the individual's economic participation or by reference to national rights. Wider debate is required to clarify the longer-term implications of this approach and whether the EU should be exploring – as part of its strategy to combat marginalisation – a more inclusive perspective which would help to integrate those who otherwise risk missing the benefits of economic progress.

NOTE

1. The three 'founding Treaties' of the European Union are the European Coal and
   Steel Community Treaty (1951), the European Economic Treaty or Treaty of Rome
   (1957) and the European Atomic Energy Community Treaty (also 1957). The
   Merger Treaty (1965) amended these founding Treaties to create one Commission
   and one Council to serve all three Communities. Since then, there have been three
   major sets of amendments to the operation of these Communities as contained in
   the Single European Act (1986), the Treaty on European Union or Maastricht
   Treaty (1992) and the Treaty of Amsterdam (1997). The constitution of the
   European Union is therefore governed by the set of all these Treaties together,
   although it should be noted that the term 'European Union' itself was not brought
   into existence formally until the Maastricht Treaty (Bainbridge 1998: 486–8).

Bibliography

Addison, J., C. Schnabel and J. Wagner (1996) 'German works councils, profits and innovation', *Kyklos*, **49** (4), 555–82.

Addison, J.T. and W.S. Siebert (1992) 'The Social Charter: whatever next?', *British Journal of Industrial Relations*, **30** (4), 495–513.

Addison, J. and J. Wagner (1997) 'The impact of German works councils on profitability and innovation: new evidence from micro data', *Jahrbücher für Nationalökonomie und Statistik*, **216** (1) (January), 1–20.

Aiginger, K. (1994) 'Sozialpartnerschaft in Österreich: theoretische Einordnung, tatsächliche Wirtschaftserfolge und Reformfähigkeit', *Wirtschaftstheoretische Blätter*, 5–6, 497–510.

Albert, M. (1991) *Capitalisme contre capitalisme* (Paris: Seuil).

Amsden, J. (1972) *Collective Bargaining and Class Conflict in Spain* (London: Weidenfeld & Nicolson).

Atkinson, A.B. (1995) 'The welfare state and economic performance', *National Tax Journal*, June, **48** (2), 171–98.

Axelrod, R. (1982) *The Evolution of Co-operation* (New York: Basic Books).

Baglioni, G. and C. Crouch (eds) (1991) *European Industrial Relations: The Challenge of Flexibility* (London: Sage Publications).

Bainbridge, T. (1998) *The Penguin Companion to the European Union* (London: Penguin Books).

Barr, N. (1992) 'Economic theory and the welfare state: a survey and interpretation', *Journal of Economic Literature*, **30** (2), 741–803.

Beardwell, I. and L. Holden (1997) *Human Resource Management: A Contemporary Perspective* (London: Pitman Publishing).

Bercusson, B., S. Deakin, P. Koistinen, Y. Kravaritou, U. Mückenberger, A. Supiot and B. Veneziani (1996) *A Manifesto for Social Europe* (Brussels: European Trade Union Institute).

Bertelsmann Stiftung/Hans-Böckler-Stiftung (1998) *Mitbestimmung und neue Unternehmenskulturen. Bilanz und Perspektiven* (Gütersloh: Verlag Bertelsmann Stiftung).

Bertold, N. and R. Fehn (1996) 'The positive economics of unemployment and labour market inflexibility', *Kyklos*, **49** (4), 583–613.

Bischof, G. and A. Pelinka (eds) (1996) *Austro-Corporatism: Past, Present, Future* (New Brunswick, NJ: Transaction Publishers).

Blair, T. (1999) *Speech to the Partners for Progress Conference*, 24 May (London: Trades Union Congress).

Blank, R. (ed.) (1994) *Social Protection versus Economic Flexibility* (Chicago: University of Chicago Press).

Blank, R. and R. Freeman (1994) 'Evaluating the Connection between Social Protection and Economic Flexibility', in R. Blank (ed.), *Social Protection versus Economic Flexibility* (Chicago: University of Chicago Press), pp. 21–42.

Blyton, P. and P. Turnbull (1998) *The Dynamics of Employee Relations* (Basingstoke: Macmillan).

BMAGS (1997) *Zielsetzungen des Österreichischen Penzionkonzeptes 2000* (Vienna: Bundesministerium für Arbeit, Gesundheit und Soziales).

BMAGS (1998) *European Social Model – Social Dialogue*, Conference Paper for the Austrian Presidency, 9–10 November (Vienna: Bundesministerium für Arbeit, Gesundheit und Soziales).

Boix, C. and D. Posner (1998) 'Social capital: explaining its origins and effects upon government performance', *British Journal of Political Science*, **28** (4), 686–93.

Breuss, F. (1993) *Herausforderungen für die Österreichische Wirtschaftspolitik und die Sozialpartnerschaft in der Wirtschafts- und Währungsunion*, Working Paper 4 (Vienna: Forschungsinstitut für Europafragen).

Bulletin of the EU (1996) 'The Jobs Challenge – Dublin Declaration on Employment', December, 12/96 (Brussels: Commission of the EC), point I.36.

Burniaux, J.-M. et al. (1998) *Income Distribution and Poverty in Selected OECD Countries*, Economics Department Working Papers no.189, March (Paris: Organisation for Economic Co-operation and Development).

Butschek, F. (1995) 'Sozialpartnerschaft aus Sicht der neuen Institutionenökonomie', *WIFO Monatsbericht* 10/95, 644–54.

Calmfors, L. and J. Driffill (1988) 'Bargaining structure, corporatism and economic performance', *Economic Policy*, 6 (April), 13–61.

Carley, M. (1993) 'Social Dialogue', in M. Gold (ed.), *The Social Dimension: Employment Policy in the European Community* (Basingstoke: Macmillan), pp. 105–34.

Carley, M. (1999) *European Social Policy Forum 98. Summary Report* (Brussels: Commission of the EC, DGV; Dublin: European Foundation for the Improvement of Living and Working Conditions).

Casey, B. (1998) 'The Costs of Youth Unemployment', in *Carnegie Young People Initiative: Good Work for Young People* (London: Youth Work Press).

Casey, B. and M. Gold (1998) *Social Dialogue in Europe: Final Report for the Bundesministerium für Arbeit, Gesundheit und Soziales*, December, mimeo.

Casey, B., E. Keep and K. Mayhew (1999) 'Flexibility, quality and competitiveness', *National Institute Economic Review*, 168 (April), 70–81.

Charkham, J. (1994) *Keeping Good Company: A Study of Corporate Governance in Five Countries* (Oxford: Oxford University Press).

Choi, K. (1983) 'A Statistical Test of Olson's Model', in D. Mueller (ed.), *The Political Economy of Growth* (New Haven, CT, and London: Yale University Press), pp. 57–78.

Clark, J. (1979) 'Concerted action in the Federal Republic of Germany', *British Journal of Industrial Relations*, 17 (2), 242–58.

Coase, R.H. (1988a) 'The Firm, the Market and the Law', in R.H. Coase, *The Firm, the Market and the Law* (Chicago and London: University of Chicago Press), pp. 1–31.

Coase, R.H. (1988b) 'The Problem of Social Cost', in R.H. Coase, *The Firm, the Market and the Law* (Chicago and London: University of Chicago Press), pp. 95–156.

Coase, R.H. (1988c) *The Firm, the Market and the Law* (Chicago and London: University of Chicago Press).

Coleman, J. (1990) *Foundations of Social Theory* (Cambridge, MA: Belknap Press of Harvard University Press).

Collins, M. and C. Kavanagh (1998) 'For Richer, for Poorer: The Changing Distribution of Household Income in Ireland, 1973–94', in S. Healy and B. Reynolds (eds), *Social Policy in Ireland: Principles, Practice and Problems* (Dublin: Oak Tree Press), pp. 163–92.

Commission (1993) *Growth, Competitiveness, Employment. The Chal-*

lenges and Ways Forward into the 21st Century. White Paper, COM (93) 700 final, 5 December (Brussels: Commission of the EC).

Commission (1994a) *European Social Policy – A Way Forward for the Union. A White Paper.* COM (94) 333 final, 27 July (Brussels: Commission of the EC).

Commission (1994b) 'Essen European Council: Conclusions of the Presidency', *Bulletin of the European Union,* December (Brussels: Commission of the EC), 7–27.

Commission (1996) *Commission Communication concerning the Development of the Social Dialogue at Community Level,* COM (96) 448 final, 18 September (Brussels: Commission of the EC).

Commission (1997a) *Modernising and Improving Social Protection in the European Union,* March (Brussels: Commission of the EC).

Commission (1997b) *Partnership for a New Organisation of Work.* Green Paper, April (Brussels: Commission of the EC).

Commission (1997c) *The 1998 Employment Guidelines. Council Resolution of 15 December 1997,* Directorate-General for Employment, Industrial Relations and Social Affairs, December (Brussels: Commission of the EC).

Commission (1998a) *From Guidelines to Action: the National Action Plans for Employment.* Communication, 13 May (Brussels: Commission of the EC).

Commission (1998b), *Adapting and Promoting the Social Dialogue at Community Level,* COM (98) 322, 20 May (Brussels: Commission of the EC [draft]).

Commission (1998c) *Status Report on the Social Dialogue 1997,* Newsletter, June (Brussels: DGV/D, Commission of the EC).

Commission (1998d), *Financing the European Union: Commission Report on the Operation of the Own Resources System,* DG XIX, 7 October (Brussels: Commission of the EC).

Commission (1998e) *1998 Employment Rates Report,* 14 October (Brussels: Commission of the EC).

Commission (1998f) *European Commission adopts 1998 Joint Employment Report,* 14 October (Brussels: Commission of the EC).

Commission (1999a) *Council Resolution on the 1999 Employment Guidelines,* February (Brussels: DGV/A, Commission of the EC).

Commission (1999b) *Community Policies in Support of Employment,*

COM (99) 167 (Brussels: Commission of the EC).

Concise Oxford Dictionary of Politics (1996) (ed. I. McLean) (Oxford: OUP).

Cooke, W. (1994) 'Employee participation, group-based incentives and company performance', *Industrial and Labor Relations Review*, **47** (4), 595–609.

Crafts, N. and G. Toniolo (eds) (1996) *Economic Growth in Europe since 1945* (Cambridge: Cambridge University Press).

Crouch, C. (1993) *Industrial Relations and European State Traditions* (Oxford: Clarendon Press).

Crouch, C. (1995) 'Reconstructing Corporatism? Organized Decentralization and Other Paradoxes', in C. Crouch and F. Traxler (eds), *Organized Industrial Relations in Europe: What Future?* (Aldershot: Avebury), pp. 311–30.

Crouch, C. and W. Streeck (1997a) 'Introduction', in C. Crouch and W. Streeck (eds), *Political Economy of Modern Capitalism: Mapping Convergence and Diversity* (London: Sage), pp. 1–18.

Crouch, C. and W. Streeck (eds) (1997b) *Political Economy of Modern Capitalism. Mapping Convergence and Diversity* (London: Sage).

Crouch, C. and F. Traxler (eds) (1995) *Organized Industrial Relations in Europe: What Future?* (Aldershot: Avebury).

Cutcher-Greshenfeld, J. (1991) 'The impact on economic performance of a transformation of industrial relations', *Industrial and Labor Relations Review*, **44** (2), 241–60.

Deininger, K. and L. Squire (1996) 'A new data set measuring income inequality', *The World Bank Economic Review*, **10** (3) (Washington, DC: The International Bank for Reconstruction and Development), 565–91.

Department of Trade and Industry (1998) *Fairness at Work*, White Paper, May, Cmnd.3968 [presented to Parliament by the President of the Board of Trade] (London: HMSO).

Due, J., J.S. Madsen and C.S. Jensen (1991) 'The social dimension: convergence or diversification of industrial relations in the Single European Market?', *Industrial Relations Journal*, **22** (2) (summer), 85–102.

Due, J., J.S. Madsen, L.K. Petersen and C.S. Jensen (1995) 'Adjusting the Danish Model: Towards Centralized Decentralization', in C. Crouch and F. Traxler (eds), *Organized Industrial Relations in Europe: What Future?* (Aldershot: Avebury), pp. 121–50.

Dyson, K. (1994) *Elusive Union. The Process of Economic and Monetary Union in Europe* (London and New York: Longman).

Economist (1999) 'Desperately seeking a perfect model', 10 April, pp. 67–9.

Eichengreen, B. (1996) 'Institutions and Economic Growth: Europe after World War II', in N. Crafts and G. Toniolo (eds), *Economic Growth in Europe since 1945* (Cambridge: Cambridge University Press), pp. 38–72.

EIRO: http://www.eiro.eurofound.ie/

Employment Department (1992) *The United Kingdom in Europe – People, Jobs and Progress*, September (London: HMSO).

Esping-Andersen, G. (1990) *The Three Worlds of Welfare Capitalism* (Cambridge: Polity).

Esping-Andersen, G. (1994) 'Welfare State and the Economy' in N.J. Smelser and R. Swedberg (eds), *The Handbook of Economic Sociology* (Princeton, NJ: Princeton University Press).

Esping-Andersen, G. (1997) 'Welfare States at the End of the Century: the Impact of Labour Market, Family and Demographic Change', in OECD (1997) *Family, Market and Community. Equity and Efficiency in Social Policy*, Social Policy Studies no. 21 (Paris: Organisation for Economic Co-operation and Development), pp. 63–80.

Esping-Andersen, G. (1999) *Social Foundations of Postindustrial Economies* (Oxford: Oxford University Press).

European Economy (1998) No. 65, Annex (Brussels: DGII, Commission of the EC).

European Works Councils Bulletin (1999) 'Article 6 state of play', issue 22, July/August (London: Industrial Relations Services; University of Warwick: Industrial Relations Research Unit), pp. 10–14.

Fajertag, G. and P. Pochet (eds) (1997) *Social Pacts in Europe* (Brussels: European Trade Union Institute).

Falkner, G. (1996) 'Sozialpolitik: Zwischen Sparpaketen und Lohndumping', in E. Tálos and G. Falkner (eds), *EU-Mitglied Österreich. Gegenwart und Perspektiven: eine Zwischenbilanz* (Vienna: Manz), pp. 239–57.

Ferner, A. and R. Hyman (1992a) 'Industrial Relations in the New Europe: Seventeen Types of Ambiguity', in A. Ferner and R. Hyman (eds), *Industrial Relations in the New Europe* (Oxford:

Blackwell), pp. xvi–xlix.

Ferner, A. and R. Hyman (eds) (1992b) *Industrial Relations in the New Europe* (Oxford: Blackwell).

Ferner, A. and R. Hyman (eds) (1998) *Changing Industrial Relations in Europe* (Oxford: Blackwell).

Fernie, S. and D. Metcalf (1995) 'Participation, contingent pay, representation and workplace performance: evidence from Great Britain', *British Journal of Industrial Relations*, 33 (3), 379–415.

Ferrara, M. (1996) 'The southern model of welfare in social Europe', *Journal of European Social Policy*, 6 (1), 17–37.

Fishbein, W.H. (1984) *Wage Restraint by Consensus: Britain's Search for an Incomes Policy Agreement, 1965–1979* (Boston, MA and London: Routledge & Kegan Paul).

Flanders, A. (1967) *Collective Bargaining: Prescription for Change* (London: Faber & Faber).

Forslund, A. and A.B. Krüger (1997) 'An Evaluation of the Swedish Active Labour Market Policy: New and Received Wisdom', in R.B. Freeman et al., *The Welfare State in Transition* (Chicago: University of Chicago Press), pp. 267–98.

Foundation of Labour (1993) *Een Nieuwe Koers* (The Hague: Stichting van der Arbeid).

Freeman, R.B. and E.P. Lazear (1995) 'An Economic Analysis of Works Councils', in J. Rogers and W. Streeck (eds), *Works Councils: Consultation, Representation and Co-operation in Industrial Relations* (Chicago: University of Chicago Press), pp. 27–50.

Freeman, R.B., R. Topel and B. Swedenborg (eds) (1997) *The Welfare State in Transition* (Chicago: University of Chicago Press).

García, S. (1992), *Europe's Fragmented Identities and the Frontiers of Citizenship*, RIIA Discussion Paper no.45 (London: Royal Institute of International Affairs).

Giebels, R. (1997) *Van 'Dutch disease' naar 'Dutch miracle' – Een verklaring voor het succes van het poldermodel*, Seminar van het Duitsland Instituut Felix Meritis te Amsterdam, 1 October (Amsterdam: Duitsland Instituut, Universiteit van Amsterdam) .

Gilbert, N. (1998) *Social Security as an Instrument for Social Cohesion: an Overview of Possibilities and Limitations*. Paper presented at the ISSA Second Technical Conference, Naples, 25–27 March (Geneva: International Social Security Association).

Giorgi, D. (1998) *L'assurance vieillesse en France. Situation et per-*

spectives. Paper presented at the ISSA Conference on the Future of Social Security, Stockholm, 29 June–1 July (Geneva: International Social Security Association).

Goetschy, J. and P. Pochet (1997) 'The Treaty of Amsterdam: a new approach to employment and social affairs', *Transfer*, **3** (3), 607–20.

Gold, M. (1993a) 'Overview of the Social Dimension', in M. Gold (ed.), *The Social Dimension: Employment Policy in the European Community* (Basingstoke: Macmillan), pp. 10–40.

Gold, M. (ed.) (1993b) *The Social Dimension. Employment Policy in the European Community* (Basingstoke: Macmillan).

Gold, M. (1998) 'Social Partnership at the EU Level: Initiatives, Problems and Implications for Member States', in D. Hine and H. Kassim (eds), *Beyond the Market: The EU and National Social Policy* (London: Routledge), pp. 107–33.

Gold, M. and M. Weiss (eds) (1999) *Employment and Industrial Relations in Europe, Vol. 1* (The Hague, London, and Boston, MA: Kluwer Law International).

Goldthorpe, J.H. (ed.) (1984) *Order and Conflict in Contemporary Capitalism* (Oxford: Clarendon Press).

Goodrich, C.L. (1975 [originally published 1920]) *The Frontier of Control: A Study in British Workshop Politics* (London: Pluto Press).

Gough, I. (1996) 'Social welfare and competitiveness', *New Political Economy*, **1** (2), 209–32.

Graham, A. (1997) 'The UK Economy 1979–95: Myths and Realities of Conservative Capitalism', in C. Crouch and W. Streeck (eds), *Political Economy of Modern Capitalism: Mapping Convergence and Diversity* (London: Sage), pp. 117–32.

Grahl, J. and P. Teague (1992) 'Integration theory and European labour markets' *British Journal of Industrial Relations*, **30** (4), 515–27.

Grant, W. (1996) 'Corporatism', in *Concise Oxford Dictionary of Politics* (ed. I. McLean) (Oxford: Oxford University Press), pp. 112–15.

Gray, A.W. (ed.) (1997) *International Perspectives on the Irish Economy* (Indecon Economic Consultants).

Gruenewald, U., D. Moraal, F. Draus, R. Weiss and D. Gnahs (1998) *Formen Arbeitsintegrierten Lernens*, QUEM-report, Heft 53 (Berlin: Arbeitsgemeinschaft Qualifikations-Entwicklungs-

Management, Geschäftsstelle der Arbeitsgemeinschaft Betriebliche Weiterbildungsforschung e.V.).

Guger, A. (1992) 'Corporatism in Austria', in J. Pekkarinen et al. (eds), *Social Corporatism: A Superior Economic System?* (Oxford: Clarendon Press/New York: Oxford University Press), pp. 338-62.

Guger, A. (1998) 'Economic policy and social democracy: The Austrian experience', *Oxford Review of Economic Policy*, **14** (1), 40-58.

Hank, R. (1996) 'Der Zauberer: "Bündnis für Arbeit" statt Programm-debatte', *Gewerkschaftliches Monatsheft*, **1996/1**, 32-40.

Hardin, R. (1982) *Collective Action* (Baltimore, MD: Johns Hopkins University Press).

Healy, S. and B. Reynolds (eds) (1998) *Social Policy in Ireland: Principles, Practice and Problems* (Dublin: Oak Tree Press).

Hemerijck, A.C. (1995) 'Corporatist Immobility in the Netherlands', in C. Crouch and F. Traxler (eds), *Organized Industrial Relations in Europe: What Future?*, pp. 183-226.

Hepple, B. (1987) 'The crisis in EEC labour law', *Industrial Law Journal*, **16**, 77-87.

Hills, J. (1993) *The Future of Welfare: A Guide to the Debate*, November (York: Joseph Rowntree Foundation).

Hine, D. and H. Kassim (eds) (1998) *Beyond the Market: The EU and National Social Policy* (London: Routledge).

Hobsbawm, E.J. (1989) *Industry and Empire: An Economic History of Britain since 1750* (London: Weidenfeld & Nicolson).

Hodges, M. and S. Woolcock (1993) 'Atlantic capitalism versus Rhine capitalism in the European Community', *West European Politics*, **16** (3) (July), 329-44.

Hostasch, L. (1998) *The European Social Model – A Social Dialogue*, press release, 9 November, Hofburg (Vienna: BMAGS).

Ingham, G.K. (1974) *Strikes and Industrial Conflict: Britain and Scandinavia* (Basingstoke: Macmillan).

Inglehart, R., M. Basañez and A. Moreno (1998) *Human Values and Beliefs: A Cross-Cultural Sourcebook: Political, Religious, Sexual and Economic Norms in 43 Societies. Findings from the 1990–1993 World Values Survey* (Ann Arbor: University of Michigan Press).

Karlhofer, F. (1996) 'The Present and Future State of Social Partnership' in G. Bischof and A. Pelinka (eds), *Austro-Corporatism: Past, Present, Future* (New Brunswick, NJ:

Transaction Publishers), pp. 119–46.

Katz, H., T. Kochan and K. Gobeille (1983) 'Industrial relations performance, economic performance and QWL programs: an interplant analysis', *Industrial and Labor Relations Review*, **37** (1), 3–17.

Katz, H., T. Kochan and J. Keefe (1987) 'Industrial relations and productivity in the U.S. automobile industry', *Brookings Papers on Economic Activity*, Vol. 3, pp. 685–715.

Katzenstein, P. (1985) *Small States in World Markets: Industrial Policy in Europe* (Ithaca, NY: Cornell University Press).

Kauppinen, T. (ed.) (1998) *The Impact of EMU on Industrial Relations in European Union*, Publication No. 9 (Helsinki: Finnish Industrial Relations Association).

Kessler, S. and F. Bayliss (1998) *Contemporary British Industrial Relations* (Basingstoke: Macmillan).

Kjellberg, A. (1998) 'Sweden: Restoring the Model?', in A. Ferner and R. Hyman (eds), *Changing Industrial Relations in Europe* (Oxford: Blackwell), pp. 74–117.

Klein, P.A. (1994) *Power and Economic Performance: The Institutionalist View* (London: Sharp).

Knack, S. and P. Keefer (1997) 'Does social capital have an economic payoff? – a cross-country investigation', *Quarterly Journal of Economics*, **112** (4), 1251–88.

Koch, M. and C. Thimann (1997) *From Generosity to Sustainability – The Austrian Pension System and Options for its Reform*, European Department/Fiscal Affairs Department, Working Paper WP/97/10 (Washington, DC: International Monetary Fund).

Kopits, G. and J. Craig (1998) *Transparency in Government Operations*, Occasional paper 158 (Washington DC: International Monetary Fund).

Korpi, W. (1978) *The Working Class in Welfare Capitalism: Work, Unions and Politics in Sweden* (London: Routledge & Kegan Paul).

Korpi, W. (1985) 'Economic growth and the welfare system: leaky bucket or irrigation system?', *European Sociological Review*, **1** (2), 97–118.

Krugman, P.R. (1997) 'Good News from Ireland. A Geographical Perspective', in A.W. Gray (ed.), *International Perspectives on the Irish Economy* (Indecon Economic Consultants) [quoted in *Financial Times*, 8 October 1998, p. 21].

Lang, K. and R. Kuhlmann (1996) ''Bündnis für Arbeit': Reform-perspektive für Vollbeschäftigung und Sozialstaat', *Gewerkschaftliches Monatsheft*, **1996/3**, 189–200.

Lange, P. (1992) 'The Politics of the Social Dimension: Interests, Rules, States and Redistribution in the 1992 Process', in A. Sbragia (ed.), *Europolitics: Institutions and Policy Making in the 'New' European Community* (Washington, DC: Brookings), pp. 225–56.

Larsson, A. (1999) 'Towards a European Pact for Employment: Address to the Social Dialogue Committee', 1 February (*Internet at* europa.eu.int/comm/dg05/speeches/990201al.html).

Lash, S. and J. Urry (1993) *The End of Organized Capitalism* (Cambridge: Polity Press).

Leibfried, S. and P. Pierson (1992) 'Prospects for social Europe', *Politics and Society*, **20** (3), 333–66.

Leibfried, S. and P. Pierson (eds) (1995) *European Social Policy: Between Fragmentation and Integration* (Washington, DC: Brookings).

Leicht, M. (1999) 'Social Capital as Competitive Advantage – Evidence from Cross-National Research', paper presented to European Sociological Congress, 'Will Europe Work?', Amsterdam, 18–21 August.

Lindbeck, A., P. Molander, T. Persson, O. Peterson, A. Sandmo, B. Swedenborg and N. Thygesen (1994) *Turning Sweden Around* (Cambridge, MA: MIT Press).

Lordon, F. (1998) 'The logic and limits of *Désinflation Compétitive*', *Oxford Review of Economic Policy*, **14** (1), 96–113.

MacDuffie, J. (1995) 'Human-resource bundles and manufacturing performance – organizational logic and flexible production systems in the world auto industry', *Industrial and Labor Relations Review*, **48** (2), 197–221.

Majone, G. (1993) 'The European Community between social policy and social regulation', *Journal of Common Market Studies*, **31** (2) (June), 153–70.

Majone, G. (1996) 'Which social policy for Europe?', in Y. Mény et al. (eds), *Adjusting to Europe: The Impact of the European Union on National Institutions and Policies* (London: Routledge), pp. 123–36.

Martín Valverde, A. (1999) 'Spain', in M. Gold and M. Weiss (eds), *Employment and Industrial Relations in Europe, Vol. I* (The Hague,

London and Boston: Kluwer Law International), pp. 191–221.

Martínez Lucio, M. (1998) 'Spain: Regulating Employment and Social Fragmentation', in A. Ferner and R. Hyman (eds), *Changing Industrial Relations in Europe* (Oxford: Blackwell), pp. 426–58.

Mény, Y., P. Muller and J.-L. Quermonne (eds) (1996a) *Adjusting to Europe: the Impact of the European Union on National Institutions and Policies* (London: Routledge).

Mény, Y., P. Muller and J.-L Quermonne (1996b) 'Introduction', in Y. Mény et al. (eds), *Adjusting to Europe: the Impact of the European Union on National Institutions and Policies* (London: Routledge), pp. 1–22.

Middlemas, K. (1980) *Politics in Industrial Society: The Experience of the British System since 1911* (London: André Deutsch).

Millward, N., M. Stevens, D. Smart and W.R. Hawes (1992) *Workplace Industrial Relations in Transition* (Aldershot: Dartmouth).

Ministry of Health and Social Affairs (1998) *Pension Reform in Sweden*, Paper presented at the ISSA Conference on the Future of Social Security, Stockholm, 29 June–1 July (Geneva: International Social Security Association).

Mitchell, D., D. Lewin and E. Lawler (1990) 'Alternative Pay Systems, Firm Performance and Productivity', in A. Blinder (ed.), *Paying for Productivity: A Look at the Evidence* (Washington, DC: Center for Economic Progress and Employment, Brookings Institution), pp. 15–88.

Morishima, M. (1991) 'Information sharing and firm performance in Japan', *Industrial Relations*, **30** (1), 37–61.

Mosley, H. and C. Degen (1994) *Reorganisation of Labour Market Policy: Further Training for the Unemployed in the United Kingdom*, Discussion Paper FS1 94–205 (Berlin: Wissenschaftszentrum Berlin für Sozialforschung).

Mosley, H., T. Keller and S. Speckesser (1998) *The Role of the Social Partners in the Design and Implementation of Active Measures*, April (Berlin: Wissenschaftszentrum Berlin für Sozialforschung).

Mueller, D. (ed.) (1983) *The Political Economy of Growth* (New Haven, CT and London: Yale University Press).

Mundo, A. (1998) *Evaluation of Social Security Reforms in Italy*, Paper presented at the European Regional Meeting on the Evaluation of Social Security Reforms, Dublin, 5–7 May (Geneva: International Social Security Association).

Myrdal, G. (1953) *The Political Element in the Development of Economic Theory* (London: Routledge & Kegan Paul).

Negrelli, S. and E. Santi (1991) 'Industrial Relations in Italy', in G. Baglioni and C. Crouch (eds), *European Industrial Relations: The Challenge of Flexibility* (London: Sage), pp. 154–98.

Negrelli, S. and T. Treu (1999) 'Italy', in M. Gold and M. Weiss (eds), *Employment and Industrial Relations in Europe, Vol.* 1 (The Hague, London and Boston: Kluwer Law International), pp. 111–41.

Neunreither, K. (1995), 'Citizens and the Exercise of Power in the European Union: Towards a New Social Contract?', in A. Rosas and E. Antola (eds), *A Citizens' Europe: In Search of a New Order* (London: Sage), pp. 1–8.

Nickell, S. (1997) 'Unemployment and labour market rigidities: Europe versus North America', *Journal of Economic Perspectives*, 11 (3) (summer), 55–74.

North, D. (1992) *Transaction Costs, Institutions and Economic Performance*, Occasional Paper No.30, International Center for Economic Growth (San Francisco, CA: ICS Press).

OECD (1981) *Integrated Social Policy. A Review of the Austrian Experience* (Paris: Organisation for Economic Co-operation and Development).

OECD (1994) *The OECD Jobs Study: Facts, Analysis, Strategies* (Paris: Organisation for Economic Co-operation and Development).

OECD (1995) *The Transition from Work to Retirement*, Social Policy Studies No.16 (Paris: Organisation for Economic Co-operation and Development).

OECD (1996) *Income Distribution in OECD Countries*, Social Policy Studies No.18 (Paris: Organisation for Economic Co-operation and Development).

OECD (1997a) *Ageing in OECD Countries. A Critical Policy Challenge*, Social Policy Studies No.20 (Paris: Organisation for Economic Co-operation and Development).

OECD (1997b) *Austria. OECD Economic Surveys* (Paris: Organisation for Economic Co-operation and Development).

OECD (1997c) 'Economic Performance and the Structure of Collective Bargaining', in *Employment Outlook 1997*, July (Paris: Organisation for Economic Co-operation and Development), 63–92.

OECD (1998a) 'Recent Labour Market Developments and Prospects', in *Employment Outlook 1998*, June (Paris: Organisation for Economic Co-operation and Development), pp. 1–30.

OECD (1998b) *United Kingdom. OECD Economic Surveys* (Paris: Organisation for Economic Co-operation and Development).

O'Leary, S. (1995) 'The Social Dimension of Community Citizenship' in A. Rosas and E. Antola (eds), *A Citizens' Europe: In Search of a New Order* (London: Sage) pp. 156–81.

Olson, M. (1995) 'The devolution of Nordic and Teutonic economies', *American Economic Review*, **85**, 22–7.

Olson, M. (1996) 'The varieties of Eurosclerosis: the rise and decline of nations since 1982', in N. Crafts and G. Toniolo (eds), *Economic Growth in Europe since 1945* (Cambridge: Cambridge University Press), pp. 73–94.

Palik, R. (1997) 'Rentenpolitik ein Dauerthema? Das Rentenreformgesetz 1999', *Soziale Sicherheit*, **11/1997**, 373–8.

Parks, S. (1995) 'Improving workplace performance: historical and theoretical contexts', *Monthly Labor Review*, **118** (5) (May), 18–28.

Pekkarinen, J., M. Pohjola and R. Rowthorn (eds) (1992a) *Social Corporatism: a Superior Economic System?* (Oxford: Clarendon Press/New York: Oxford University Press).

Pekkarinen, J., M. Pohjola and R. Rowthorn (1992b) 'Social Corporatism and Economic Performance: Introduction', in J. Pekkarinen et al. (eds), *Social Corporatism: a Superior Economic System?* (Oxford: Clarendon Press/New York: Oxford University Press), pp. 1–23.

Pelinka, A., C. Schaller, H. Sickinger and B. Unger (1998) *Social Dialogue in Europe: Final Report*, September (Vienna: Institut für Konfliktforschung).

Pelling, H. (1992) *A History of British Trade Unionism* (Basingstoke: Macmillan).

Pestoff, V.A. (1995) 'Towards a New Swedish Model of Collective Bargaining and Politics' in C. Crouch and F. Traxler (eds), *Organized Industrial Relations in Europe: What Future?* (Aldershot: Avebury), pp. 151–82.

Pochet, P. (1998) 'EMU and Industrial Relations: An Overview of National Debates', in T. Kauppinen (ed.), *The Impact of EMU on Industrial Relations in European Union*, Publication No. 9

(Helsinki: Finnish Industrial Relations Association), pp. 262–76.

Pochet, P. and G. Fajertag (1997) 'Social Pacts in Europe in the 1990s. Towards a European Social Pact?', in G. Fajertag and P. Pochet (eds), *Social Pacts in Europe* (Brussels: European Trade Union Institute), pp. 9–25.

Pollan, W. (1997) 'Political Exchange in Austria's Collective Bargaining System: the Role of the Nationalised Industries', in M. Sverke (ed.), *The Future of Trade Unionism: International Perspectives on Emerging Union Structures* (Aldershot: Ashgate), pp. 47–62.

Presidency (1999) 'European Employment Pact: Closer Co-operation to Boost Employment and Economic Reforms in Europe. Annex to the Presidency Conclusions – Cologne European Council': Internet at http://www.europa.eu.int/council/off/conclu/june99/june99_en.pdf

Pribyl, H. (1991) *Sozialpartnerschaft in Österreich (mit einer Einführung von Alfred Klose)* (Vienna: A. Schendl).

Putnam, R. (1993) *Making Democracy Work: Civic Traditions in Modern Italy* (Princeton, NJ: Princeton University Press).

Recio, A. and J. Roca (1998) 'The Spanish Socialists in power: thirteen years of economic policy', *Oxford Review of Economic Policy*, **14** (1) (spring).

Regalia, I. and M. Regini (1998) 'Italy: the Dual Character of Industrial Relations', in A. Ferner and R. Hyman (eds), *Changing Industrial Relations in Europe* (Oxford: Blackwell), pp. 459–503.

Reithofer, H. (1995) *Sozialpolitik in Österreich: Probleme, Lösungen, Argumente. Eine Praxisorientierte Darstellung* (Vienna: Verlag des Österreichischen Gewerkschaftsbundes).

Rhodes, M. (1998) 'Defending the Social Contract: The EU between Global Constraints and Domestic Imperatives', in D. Hine and H. Kassim (eds), *Beyond the Market: The EU and National Social Policy* (London: Routledge), pp. 36–59.

Roach, S. (1998) 'Europe's dilemmas revisited', *Financial Times*, 27 May.

Rodrik, D. (1997), *Where Did All the Growth Go? External Shocks, Social Conflict and Growth Collapses* (Cambridge, MA: John F. Kennedy School of Government), November; mimeo.

Rogers, J. and W. Streeck (eds) (1995) *Works Councils: Consultation, Representation and Co-operation in Industrial Relations* (Chicago and London: Chicago University Press).

Rosas, A. and E. Antola (eds) (1995), *A Citizens' Europe: In Search of*

142   *Social Partnership and Economic Performance*

a New Order (London: Sage).

Rösner, H.J. (1996) 'Bündnis für Arbeit – ist Korporativismus noch zeitgemäss?', *Wirtschaftsdienst*, **1996/III**, 122–30.

Rowthorn, R. (1992) 'Corporatism and Labour Market Performance', in J. Pekkarinen et al. (eds), *Social Corporatism: A Superior Economic System?* (Oxford: Clarendon Press/New York: Oxford University Press), pp. 52–131.

Santer, J. (1996) 'Speech to Tripartite Conference on Growth and Employment', Rome, 14 June, in Bulletin of the EU (1996) *Action for Employment in Europe. A Confidence Pact*, Supplement 4/96 (Brussels: Commission of the EC), 7-10.

Sbragia, A. (ed.) (1992) *Europolitics: Institutions and Policy Making in the 'New' European Community* (Washington, DC: Brookings).

Scharpf, F. (1999) *Governing in Europe: Effective and Democratic?* (Oxford: Oxford University Press).

Schlecht, O. (1997) 'Ist Deutschland noch zu Reformen fähig?', *Wirtschaftsdienst*, **1997/X**, 555-60.

Schmaehl, W. (1993) 'The "1992" reform of public pensions in Germany: main elements and some effects', *Journal of European Social Policy*, **3** (1), 35-51.

Schmitter, P.C. (1974) 'Still the century of corporatism?', *Review of Politics*, **36**, 85-131.

Schmitter, P.C. and J.R. Grote (1997) 'Der korporatistische Sysiphus: Vergangenheit, Gegenwart, Zukunft', *Politische Vierteljahresschrift*, **38** (3), 530-54.

SER Bulletin (1997) 'Terug naar Wassenaar', December, 3-15.

Sinclair, P. and N. Horsewood (1997) *Has the Phillips Curve Been Reborn?*, Working Paper RSC 97/41 (Florence: European University Institute).

Smelser, N.J. and R. Swedberg (eds) (1994) *The Handbook of Economic Sociology* (Princeton, NJ: Princeton University Press).

Soskice, D. (1990) 'Wage determination: the changing role of institutions in advanced industrialised countries', *Oxford Review of Economic Policy*, **6**, 36-61.

Soskice, D. (1996) *German Technology Policy, Innovation and National Institutional Frameworks*, Discussion Paper FS 1 96-319 (Berlin: Wissenschaftszentrum Berlin für Sozialforschung).

SPD, Bündnis 90/Die Grünen (1998) *Aufbruch und Erneuerung – Deutschlands Weg ins 21. Jahrhundert: Koalitionsvereinbarung zwischen der Sozialdemokratischen Partei Deutschlands und Bündnis 90/Die Grünen*, 20 October (Bonn: SPD, Bündnis 90/Die Grünen).

Streeck, W. (1992a) 'Productive Constraints: On the Institutional Conditions of Diversified Production' in W. Streeck, *Social Institutions and Economic Performance* (London: Sage), pp. 1–40.

Streeck, W. (1992b) 'Co-determination: After Four Decades', in W. Streeck, *Social Institutions and Economic Performance* (London: Sage), pp. 137–68.

Streeck, W. (1992c) *Social Institutions and Economic Performance* (London: Sage).

Sverke, M. (ed.) (1997) *The Future of Trade Unionism: International Perspectives on Emerging Union Structures* (Aldershot: Ashgate).

SZW (1996) *The Dutch Welfare State from an International and Economic Perspective* (The Hague: Ministerie van Sociale Zaken en Werkgelegenheid).

SZW (1997) *Social Policy and Economic Performance* (The Hague: Ministerie van Sociale Zaken en Werkgelegenheid).

Tabatabai, H. (1996) *Statistics on Poverty and Income Distribution. An ILO Compendium of Data* (Geneva: International Labour Organisation).

Tálos, E. and G. Falkner (eds) (1996) *EU-Mitglied Österreich. Gegenwart und Perspektiven: eine Zwischenbilanz* (Vienna: Manz).

Tálos, E. and K. Wörister (1994) *Soziale Sicherung im Sozialstaat Österreich: Entwicklung, Herausforderungen, Strukturen* (Baden-Baden: Nomos-Verlag-Gesellschaft).

Taylor, R. (1998a) 'Blair confronts union chiefs across their line in the sand', *Financial Times*, 31 March.

Taylor, R. (1998b) 'Fairness at work', *Financial Times*, 20 May, p. 12.

Thompson, L. (1998) *Older and Wiser: The Economics of Public Pensions* (Washington, DC: The Urban Institute Press).

Thurow, L. (1993) *Head to Head: The Coming Battle among Japan, Europe and America* (New York: Morrow).

Tomandl, T. and K. Fürböck (1986) *Social Partnership. The Austrian System of Industrial Relations and Social Insurance* (Cornell: ILR Press).

Traxler, F. (1995a) 'Farewell to Labour Market Institutions? Organized versus Disorganized Decentralization as a Map for Industrial Relations' in C. Crouch and F. Traxler (eds), *Organized Industrial*

Relations in Europe: What Future? (Aldershot: Avebury), pp. 3–19.

Traxler, F. (1995b) 'From Demand-side to Supply-side Corporatism? Austria's Labour Relations and Public Policy', in C. Crouch and F. Traxler (eds), *Organized Industrial Relations in Europe: What Future?* (Aldershot: Avebury), pp. 271–86.

Traxler, F. (1997) 'The Logic of Social Pacts', in G. Fajertag and P. Pochet (eds), *Social Pacts in Europe* (Brussels: European Trade Union Institute), pp. 27–36.

Traxler, F. (1998) 'Austria: Still the Country of Corporatism', in A. Ferner and R. Hyman (eds), *Changing Industrial Relations in Europe* (Oxford: Blackwell), pp. 239–61.

Tsoukalis, L. (1997) *The New European Economy Revisited* (Oxford: Oxford University Press).

UNDP (1990) *Human Development Report*, United Nations Development Programme (New York: Oxford University Press).

Unger, B. (1998) *Room for Manoeuvre. Choices Left for National Economic Policy* (Vienna: Wirtschaftsuniversität), Habilitationsschrift (University thesis), mimeo.

Van der Heijden, P. (1999) 'The Netherlands' in M. Gold and M. Weiss (eds), *Employment and Industrial Relations in Europe, Vol. 1* (The Hague, London and Boston, MA: Kluwer Law International), pp. 143–66.

Van Empel, F. (1997) *Model Holland: The Power of Consultation*, (The Hague: Stichting van de Arbeid), September.

Van Steenbergen, B. (1994a) 'The Condition of Citizenship: An Introduction' in B. Van Steenbergen (ed.), *The Condition of Citizenship* (London: Sage), pp. 1–9.

Van Steenbergen, B. (ed.) (1994b) *The Condition of Citizenship* (London: Sage).

Van Waarden, F. (1997) 'Institutions of Socio-Economic Co-ordination: A European Style?', in *Social Policy and Economic Performance: Summary* (The Hague: Ministerie van Sociale Zaken en Werkgelegenheid), pp. 49–93.

Vartiainen, J. (1998) 'Understanding Swedish Social Democracy: victims of success?', *Oxford Review of Economic Policy*, **14** (1), 19–37.

Visser, J. (1991) 'Continuity and Change in Dutch Industrial Relations', in G. Baglioni and C. Crouch (eds), *European*

Industrial Relations: The Challenge of Flexibility (London: Sage), pp. 199–242.

Visser, J. (1998) 'The Netherlands: The Return of Responsive Corporatism' in A. Ferner and R. Hyman (eds), *Changing Industrial Relations in Europe* (Oxford: Blackwell), pp. 283–314.

Visser, J. and A. Hemerijck (1997), *'A Dutch Miracle': Job Growth, Welfare Reform and Corporatism in the Netherlands* (Amsterdam: University of Amsterdam Press).

Williamson, O.E. (1975) *Markets and Hierarchies: Analysis and Antitrust Implications: A Study in the Economics of Internal Organization* (New York: Free Press).

Williamson, O.E. (1993) *The Economic Analysis of Institutions and Organisations – in General and with Respect to Country Studies*, OECD Economics Department Working Papers (Paris: Organisation for Economic Co-operation and Development).

Wirtschaftskammer Österreich (1997) *Wirtschaftsstandort Österreich* (Vienna: Abteilung für Statistik), October.

Index

Addison, J.T. 81
Albert, M. 15
America *see* United States
Atkinson, A.B. 18, 84, 89
Austria
  collective bargaining 1–2, 40
  economic performance 93, 94, 95,
    96, 98
  employee relations, negotiations
    41, 47, 49, 50, 72
  governance 14, 24, 25
  labour market training 54, 58, 60
  macroeconomic policy formulation,
    and social partnership 26, 28,
    29–30, 35–6, 37, 72
  National Action Plan on
    employment 112, 113
  pay determination 39, 40, 41, 47,
    49, 50, 53, 72
  social partnership in 23, 122
  social protection in 16, 62, 64, 65,
    68, 69, 70–71, 72
  vocational training in 53, 54, 60, 72

Barr, N. 6
Beardwell, I. 48
Bertold, N. 124
Blank, R. 80
Blyton, P. 104
Boix, C. 4
Breuss, F. 91
Burniaux, J.-M. 18
Butschek, F. 91

Calmfors, L. 19
Carley, M. 121, 123
Casey, B. 7, 84

centralisation
  and economic performance 86–7
  in pay and employee relations 39,
    40, 41–4, 77
Charkham, J. 33
Choi, K. 79
Clark, J. 34, 35
Coase, R.H. 3–4
collective bargaining
  centralised 39, 40, 41–4, 77
  decentralised 40, 44–52, 77, 104
  and economic performance 86–7,
    88
  levels 40, 104–5
  statistics 1–2
  see also employee relations; pay
    determination
Collins, M. 18
conditions of service *see* employee
  relations
Cooke, W. 83
corporatism 11–12, 14
  and economic performance 86–7,
    98–101, 108
  and labour market training 58–9
  pressures on 77
  and social protection 63, 65
  in the United Kingdom 30
  see also supply-side corporatism
Craig, J. 88
Crouch, C. 20, 107
Cutcher-Greshenfeld, J. 82

decentralisation
  of collective bargaining 40, 44–52,
    77, 104
  and economic performance 86–7